Ben —
I hope you enjoy this
book and see Nicaragua as
an example of how the
worlds of work, faith and
service can be intertwined.

Pet

PS - I have access to
a color version of
this photo :)

Praise for

Reversing Burnout
How to Immediately Engage Top Talent and Grow!

In this crazy mach-5, over-caffeinated and hyper-connected culture we live in, burnout is inevitable. Not just for the CEOs and high-performing leaders but more and more it's happening across every level of our organizations. It is one of the biggest reasons that job satisfaction and engagement is at an all-time low. It prevents us from hiring, developing and retaining our best talent! Peter nails how to address burnout in your own life and gives you the tools and behaviors that will cure burnout in your organization. Thank you for writing this Pete, and I will be recommending your book to all of the leaders that I coach!

~ John Ramstead
CEO and Founder of Beyond Influence, Inc.
and the Eternal Leadership Podcast
Executive Coach and preferred leadership training
for the U.S. Military

Reversing Burnout is the must read for business professionals of our time. Written with the precision of the engineer that Pete is plus the very human touch that defines his work and life, this is a critical tool and strategy for professionals everywhere. Anyone who has experienced even small amounts of burnout will find this the comprehensive guide out. Written through the eyes of someone who has made the journey and has created a new and better world, it is without doubt the finest guide I have seen. Keep it near you all of your business life. You won't be sorry.

~ Ralph Twombly
Founder of Priority Learning
www.prioritylearningresearch.com

Reversing Burnout is a remarkably insightful read as to the very real epidemic of disengagement and burnout and its tremendous impact on businesses, corporations and hospitals alike. Peter's experience and dissection of the issues so very accurately defines and describes the problems and also provides a clear and concise pathway toward retaining and growing talent, as well as helping oneself to re-pivot for a personally fulfilling and healthy career. This is a must read for any professional and any organization's administration and leadership.

~ Marc Hodroff, MD
Founding Partner
Fore River Urology

In the legal profession, the concept of burnout is well-established. As a managing partner for a top 20 law firm, I found Pete's book to be insightful and it hit close to home. Pete's insight, analysis, and reflections help me see the trends in our firm and with myself. While I was in the middle of reading the book, one of our senior attorneys gave their notice after spending years as the director of one of our more profitable programs. In discussing the departure, the word "burnout" was cited multiple times. While it is too late to salvage that relationship, this book gave me the tools to recognize warning signs and the knowledge to take steps to hopefully avoid losing other members while being able to attract and retain future talent.

~ Thomas Quartararo, Esq.
Senior Partner/ Director,
Robinson, Kriger & McCallum

Pete has managed to provide sound and practical guidance to a topic that too often falls prey to lip service and jingoism. A winning argument for a balanced approach to managing talent in today's workplace.

~ Patrick Sweeney
CFO and senior executive
for multiple national and multinational companies

This was a great book to read from a Human Resources standpoint. The topic of burnout can sometimes be a difficult one for employees to talk about in this work climate. If employees see management being more open to discuss and see signs ahead of time and work on changes, this will make for a better workforce not only at your company but also in that employee's personal life. This book hits on some major themes, thoughts, and positive ways to make changes.

~ Chad Smithers
Human Resources Manager
A2H - Engineers • Architects • Planners

I read Peter Atherton's book, *Reversing Burnout*, with great interest. Much like many Gen Xers, I am now at the stage of life where I feel I have proven myself and it is time to look at the big picture of my life. A couple of years ago I said to my wife, "I am not yet at the 'burnout' stage but I can see it in the horizon." Peter's book was just what I needed to read. It guided me to affirm where I am in this stage of life, how I can help the 90 employees in my corrugated box company, and how to do all of that while still running a successful business. It is not an easy task, but it is one that, with Peter's book as my reference guide, I feel much more confident that I can handle the challenge. Thank you for writing this book!

~ Derek Volk
President of Volk Packaging Corporation
and author of *Chasing the Rabbit: A Dad's Life Raising a Son on the Spectrum*

Through this thought-provoking narrative of Pete's own experiences with burnout, I am forced to consider my own career burnout. His original I.M.P.A.C.T. process will help you immediately move forward and avoid disengagement. Pete gives insightful tools to gauge where we lie on the burnout spectrum and helps with reversing the burnout.

~ Jeffrey Messer
President
Messer Truck Equipment

Pete Atherton is a rare breed of entrepreneur. Most are bottom-line focused, and there's nothing wrong with that! However, with this important book, you too will discover that Pete has put his money where his mouth – and heart – is by leaving a high-paying executive position to help more leaders and companies with a perplexing and growing problem – burnout.

Reversing Burnout – How to Immediately Engage Top Talent and Grow takes a fresh look at the problem, and also gives several new and well thought out strategies that in my opinion can be easily implemented and make a real and lasting difference, beginning today.

In full disclosure, Pete is not only a friend but a coaching client. When Pete shared his idea for this book, my first reaction was, "This can't be another book that just talks about burnout!" And to his credit, Pete didn't do that – he provided us an answer to it. Through the experience he has as a leader, and more importantly, as a visionary, I see clearly why Pete left his executive position to help far more companies than just his former understand what top talent wants and lead them in creating solutions that ultimately help companies grow and prosper.

Pete is passionate about solving this problem and has made helping others win at both work and life his new focus. I applaud his efforts and after reading this book, you will as well.

~ Jim Palmer
The Dream Business Coach
www.GetJimPalmer.com

Reversing Burnout

How to Immediately Engage Top Talent and Grow!
A Blueprint for Professionals and Business Owners

By Peter C. Atherton, P.E.

President and Founder, ActionsProve, LLC

Reversing Burnout
How to Immediately Engage Top Talent and Grow!
A Blueprint for Professionals and Business Owners

Published by ActionsProve Publishing
PO Box 1267
Knoxville, TN 37901

ISBN: 978-0-9996712-0-7

Cover design by Jim Saurbaugh, JS Graphic Design

DISCLAIMER AND/OR LEGAL NOTICES
     While the publisher and authors have used their best efforts in preparing this book, they make no representations or warranties with respect to the accuracy or completeness of the contents of this book. The advice and strategies contained herein may not be suitable for your situation. You should consult a professional where appropriate. Neither the publisher nor the authors shall be liable for any loss of profit or any other commercial damages, including but not limited to special, incidental, consequential, or other damages. The purchaser or reader of this publication assumes responsibility for the use of these materials and information. Adherence to all applicable laws and regulations, both advertising and all other aspects of doing business in the United States or any other jurisdiction, is the sole responsibility of the purchaser or reader.

     This book is intended to provide accurate information with regards to the subject matter covered. However, the Author and the

This book is dedicated to my wife and kids: That they pursue excellence and a full life, and have impact in what they are called to do and for those they are called to serve.

Table of Contents

Acknowledgments

I want to thank my parents, my wife, and my children, as well as my extended family and friends who have encouraged me to pursue a full life with conviction, enthusiasm, and excitement. I also want to thank all those who have modelled excellence and authenticity at work and in life – especially those who have done so with a true servant's heart. This includes Ralph Merrill who was instrumental in catapulting my "parallel life."

With this book, and my work through ActionsProve, I hope to pay this all forward with a spirit of gratitude. I also hope to attain standing that I have done and will do well with all that I am given, and will be able to impact all those I am called to serve.

To your winning,

Pete

Preface

"What just happened should inspire and cause fear." That's what I have heard from so many friends, fellow professionals, and business owners over the past year or so. It should *inspire* individuals to take ownership and begin to live the full life they have dreamed of – but feel blocked from. It should cause every executive and management team to pause and then *fear* maintaining the status quo.

In some ways, it makes no sense for someone at the peak of their career to walk away from an executive position and large sums of near guaranteed money to begin anew. But that is an old, conventional way of thinking. In the new, it makes perfect sense.

We are living in a new age, but too many of us have been too busy to notice. Furthermore, too many of us have been sidelined by burnout and disengagement from unevolved workplaces and an inability to participate. I needed a timeout experience, a parallel life, a lot of great counsel, and a little tough love, but entering and participating in the new has made all the difference.

My heart breaks when I see so many still trapped, feeling defeated, and unable to share all the skills, talents, assets, and gifts they have and want to offer. The good news is that the tide has shifted, and the new flows in favor of top talent. Top leaders and organizations embracing this shift and designing systems to align also gain favor and benefit.

This book employs an engineering approach to present the promise and the opportunities of the new. As engineering is the practical application of science, this book is the practical application of the new to reverse burnout, immediately engage top talent, and grow. This book speaks specifically to us in terms of the "many hats" we must wear as professionals and business owners. This book is designed like a funnel to allow us to thoroughly understand the realities of work and life today and then move us toward defined goals and destinations. The book then presents a blueprint and an engineered process we, as individuals, organizations, and leaders, can use for winning... and along the way transform the American workplace for the benefit of us all.

Please accept this invitation to the new.

Welcome to the New

The old ways are no longer working. Conventional thinking is not only ineffective today, it has resulted in damage and loss… to both individuals and to organizations. The harm has been out-matched, however, and the result has a steady migration by top talent toward a better future. Whether or not we have fully recognized it, "business as usual" has been disrupted, and the disruption is only picking up in intensity and reach.

There is a growing epidemic of burnout and disengagement in the workplace today. As a result, many professionals and other high achievers are leaving or poised to leave successful careers… to pivot away. Maybe it's because work is just too consuming too much of the time – leaving us with very little time or energy for other things. Maybe our careers don't provide us the growth and excitement they once did. Or, maybe we are just at the point in life where we want more – greater meaning and purpose and more fulfillment. No matter the reason, something's gotta give. Individuals, organizations, and even industries are struggling, trying to make sense of it. We all need an answer. I wrote this book to provide one.

This book details a new way for top talent and organizations to understand burnout in order to reverse it but also to address it in such a way that immediately engages employees in what they are looking for and positions both individuals and organizations for greater growth and success.

Redefining Success

As soon as I saw the graphic, I understood. It instantly articulated what had happened to me, and I saw the connection. Sitting in a leadership conference in 2016, it had been about five years since I'd decided to pivot my career and one month since I'd sold my company stock and resigned from the Board of Directors. I'd held that position for 13 years, joining the Board and becoming vice president at age 32.

For the first 20 years of my career, I was an achiever. I wanted to achieve. I worked hard. I took on assignments. I made sure they were completed and correct. I asked what else I could do. I had goals that would lead to more learning, more responsibility, more advancement, and more rewards. Sound familiar?

My first major career milestone was to become a professional engineer. I checked off that box in 1998. Later that year, my professional career took me from a large, globally recognized engineering firm in Boston to a then much smaller and lesser known firm in Maine. The new firm actually dared to tell me I could reach whatever level of success I wanted so long as I proved myself capable. Wow. I was on my way. The combination of my drive and having no boundaries fueled me on to an accelerated path to success that felt great, really great... right up until it didn't.

Despite all the achievements, there came a point when I sensed a change happening. My interests in continuing on the path I was on began to decelerate. I learned this downshifting was real two years later, and I shared with the partners at my firm that I'd be doing something different in five to ten years. I wrote the words, and the reality was that I had no idea exactly what I'd be doing, but I was certain it was not going to be more of the same.

It wasn't just burnout from a career that I now realized took as much as it gave. I was also beginning to resent aspects of the work that had been such a big part of my life and the basis for my success. I knew my engineering work was good, even honorable, but I was discontented. As I began seeking more from life, barriers became evident.

How much life can be had after I put in my routine 45 to 50 hours at the office or on the road and checking emails before I went to bed and as I woke up? How much life can be had when Saturday mornings were spent catching up on the past workweek and Sunday evenings were planning for the week to come? The barriers raised questions that seemed all too common; the answers, however, would require something new. Ultimately, and at what was seemingly the peak of my career, I needed to choose between where I was and where I wanted to go. I chose a career pivot, but it didn't need to be that way.

The Game Plan

This book is segmented into three sections. The first section reveals what we need to understand about the realities of work and life today for many professionals and business owners. For those of us already experienced in the workforce, this section will help you understand the causes of burnout and disengagement you or your top employees may be feeling and why career pivoting has become so appealing. For those newer to the workforce, this section will help you understand some of the traps and pitfalls that have affected so many of us who have come before you and better position you to design a successful career that is balanced and integrated with greater meaning and purpose and more overall fulfillment. Understanding this information will also make you a more informed employment seeker.

The second section of the book defines what top talent wants today. This section is important for many of us who want to begin to reverse burnout and need to set an initial target toward a new future. This section is also important for organizational leaders who want to better understand the elements that will help employees reverse burnout and be able to thrive again in the workplace.

The final section of the book serves as a blueprint for professionals and business owners to reverse burnout, immediately engage top talent, and grow in ways that are right for you and your organization. The blueprint allows leaders to tackle the realities of work and life today in ways that align with what top employees want. The role of good leadership to the success of any initiative related to reversing burnout cannot be overstated. As such, I have devoted a full chapter to describing the kind of leadership that is necessary to achieve this outcome and set the stage for greater growth and success.

The Answer

The answer to reversing burnout, engaging top talent, and growing is in understanding and embracing the new realities of today; changing and expanding our mindsets, perspectives, and experiences; and being part of work and a work environment that supports, encourages, and enables winning at both work and life.

There is no quick fix for burnout or disengagement. Achieving a positive outcome requires personal and organizational ownership to begin, followed by working through a process. We need to be willing and able to take the time needed to solve the problems that led to them. Taking time is only the first step. We need to be willing and able to learn about and understand all the root causes and contributing elements of burnout and disengagement – and then discern what that means for us, or for us and our organizations.

The answer to reversing burnout, engaging top talent, and growing is as much a process as it is a series of specific actions toward a resolution. As such, just knowing the answer and understanding the engineered processes presented in this book is of limited value without having the knowledge of how best to apply them as part of a well-designed and coordinated plan to win.

We can think about reversing burnout, engaging top talent, and growing in the context of eating right and exercising. Knowing that we should eat right and exercise doesn't mean we do them – and doing them doesn't mean we do them consistently or successfully over the long term to realize their benefits. Despite the undisputed importance of eating right and exercising, we often fall short until we reach the point of owning the outcome we desire and figuring out how to make it all work for our lives and our circumstances. We can also think about reversing burnout, engaging top talent, and growing in the context of running a marathon. Attempting to run a marathon without having and following a well-designed and effective training plan that works with your life and your circumstances is not credible and not likely to lead to finishing or finishing well.

The life most of us are experiencing today is much different than the past. The realities of work and life have changed rapidly, and our busyness has made matters worse. Burnout and disengagement is costing us and our organizations and creating fewer winners at work and in life. We know this is wrong. We know we don't want this kind of life for ourselves... and we don't want it for our kids or others we care about. The problem seems so big that we just don't know what to do. We feel trapped and are most often offered only the choice to suck it up until we can leave or pivot away on our own terms – or until we just can't take it anymore. This is **not** what we dreamed for our lives, and these are **not** the conditions indicative of good leadership. We need a change. We need the courage to do what it takes to win today. We need to take a stand. We need to transform the American workplace.

The life and career we thought was too good to be true is not. Welcome to the new.

Part 1:

The Realities of Work and Life Today

The demands of work and life today are much different than they were even 10 or 20 years ago. Today, many of us feel burned-out, busy, and trapped. Sometimes we're not sure if we can keep up the current pace for another *year*, let alone another 10, 20, or 30 years, and we are often not even sure we are headed in the right direction.

For many of us, especially those of us who are professionals and business owners, the world seems to have changed around us. We have been participants in many of the changes in technology, mobile access, and social media. We're now connected virtually all the time from virtually anywhere on any of our devices. Even if we have not yet participated, most of us are at least aware of the major societal shifts toward wanting greater meaning and purpose and wanting our lives to matter more.

The problem for many of us is not the change. These changes have the power to make our lives easier, allow us to be better connected, and provide us a larger platform to make our mark and to have impact. The problem for many of us is that we have not had the time nor the perspective to process these changes and then leverage them for our benefit. We have been too busy building our careers and businesses and raising our families.

Compounding the changes around us is the fact that many of us have also changed. Many of us have shifted into new work and life seasons – and some of us may not have even realized it. Our interests, goals, and passions change with our seasons. When we are operating out of sync with our season, the feelings of burnout, busyness, and being trapped are often magnified.

If we are going to solve the problem of chronic burnout, busyness, and feeling trapped, we need both focus and commitment. We need these because those feelings of burnout, busyness, and being trapped are not even the real problems! Although problematic, they are only symptoms. The actual problems are much deeper, and they transcend conventional work and life boundaries and status quo management structures.

Perspectives from Experience

For over 20 years, I have been a near rabid consumer of personal success and leadership development materials. Before podcasts, weekly blogs, and access through social media, I was devouring available books and books-on-tape. Early in my career, these books and tapes were very encouraging and provided answers that helped me achieve the success I was striving for. When I was first dealing with burnout and realizing that I was also going through a major life transformation, I had a much harder time finding answers.

In order to find the answers I wanted and needed, I had to pull from many different sources. I also needed to intentionally spend time processing how these pieces from various sources fit together in the context of my career and my experiences. It was a very iterative process. Once I found information and processed it, I realized more was needed and the cycle repeated. This process continued for a number of years. As an engineer, my interests and training has been geared toward problem solving. I was about results. I was about practical applications. I didn't seek a research grant, I sought answers for my life, and I wanted those answers as fast as possible, so I could put them into practice.

My first order of business was to define and understand the problems that needed to be solved – an ingrained engineering approach.

Understanding these problems was not simply about understanding how they manifest in symptoms but in their underlying causes. This first section of the book brings to light the problems that underlie the symptoms of burnout, busyness, and feelings of being trapped that we are experiencing today. Later sections will outline what top employees are looking for today and present a blueprint for helping both individuals and organizations grow and prosper by addressing and solving the causes.

Chapter One

Burnout and Disengagement

Busy. Hustling. Over-committed. Over-connected. Exhausted. No *real* end in sight. It's the feeling many of us share. Not only is there always one more project to complete, one more proposal to write, one more report to submit, or a dozen or more emails to read, there's one more quarter or 100-day plan to show results, and one more year to finish up strong. That project, quarter, and year suddenly turns into a decade of "work busy" before we know it. On top of this "work busy" we are also often "life busy."

Feeling burnout is a process and can be the result of a singular or combination of work and life stresses. This chapter walks through the causes and mechanics of burnout and disengagement today.

Commitment, Ownership, and Excellence

Achieving goals we desire can energize, motivate, and inspire us to accomplish great things, things that most others don't or won't do, and things that we may not have previously thought possible. Commitment to those goals we desire helps build our character and self-esteem. It is commitment to goals that *do not* line up with our present needs or our desired future that can contribute to burnout.

Commitment is vital to establishing ourselves as successful professionals and business owners. All we've needed to do to achieve our goals is embedded in our story and helps define who we are today. Whatever motivated us to become a professional or a business owner – the challenge, the paycheck, the standing in society, or the expectations of others – a full commitment was necessary. And wherever we are right now in our careers, we need to begin our understanding of present-day burnout and disengagement with the realization that our commitment to our career started long before our first day on the job – and for some of us, our commitment dates back to high school.

Early on, we needed to take ownership to target a direction for our lives and focus our time to realize our future. We needed to select a school and a major. We needed to get through 8:00 a.m. classes and a more challenging curriculum than many of our friends. We needed to secure and succeed in internships and residencies, and we needed to pass all-day tests or licensures or certifications. At some point, however, many of us lost some ownership in the details and the direction in our lives.

For many of us, we also desired to make a difference and contribute to the greater good. We wanted to find that "thing" (or "things") unique to us at which we can excel. In addition to allowing us to provide value, we knew that those "things" would also help us feel valued, appreciated, and connected with others. This can be as basic as being a good mom, dad, coach, or friend. However, our desire to contribute doesn't always stop at good. Most of us are

> *Our desire to contribute doesn't stop at good; most of us want to excel.*

more ambitious and we want to excel, be great...and even be world-class – on both personal and professional levels.

18

When we began our careers, we entered a new season. We needed to confirm our career choice as we committed to the goals of our new employers. Individually, our commitment was most likely to excel and have impact in our chosen field: to create things and access (for those in engineering), to provide means and opportunities (for those in sales, marketing, accounting, finance, and education), to produce processes and justice (for those in law), and to advance health and wellness (for those in medicine)... just to name a few.

For virtually all professions, excelling and achieving standing and having success requires us to be "all in" for an extended period – often 10, 20, or even 30 years. This may be exactly what it takes to master our craft, make a name, and build our platform. Success as a professional is as much or more about applied knowledge than it is information alone. We need to make judgments. We need to operate in gray areas. To get to this point, we need to gain both experience and understanding. There is no other way to do this than to spend the appropriate amount of time in our craft to learn, do, fail, seek more opportunities, and repeat. The more time and the more focus, the more growth – and the quicker

> *It takes commitment and time to master our respective crafts.*

the path to success. There is so much to learn on the job, especially in the early years, and your commitment to do so can be consuming. This can be consuming in a positive and productive way... but this can also work against us. Over time, our commitment to our careers through our craft can cause us to lose touch with ourselves and others, lose track of our accomplishments, and lose clarity of where things may be heading.

We want our doctors, lawyers, engineers, financial gurus, nurses, and teachers to at least excel, if not be great or world-class. If not, we are disappointed. And we expect them to be clear and focused on serving us, as our clients, customers, and patients expect us to be serving them. This is why professionals have prominent standing in our communities. Having this prominence and being able to positively contribute in these chosen fields is often part of what drove our commitment to excel or become great, or world-class in the first place. Achieving this standing took ownership to leverage our time, interests, and passions and commitment to persevere. For many of us, this helped build our self-esteem and confidence. It was ***not*** our commitment to learning and mastering our craft where the seeds of burnout and disengagement were planted. Those seeds were

> *Intervening factors, not our pursuit of excellence alone, causes burnout.*

planted elsewhere. In fact, the opposite is true. Being able to continually grow and excel can actually help to reverse burnout and re-engage.

Yes, it takes commitment to become both a successful professional and business owner. Yes, it takes commitment to learn to excel, be great, or be world-class. And, yes, most professionals and business owners carry heavy workloads. However, unless there are intervening factors, commitment to excellence itself will not result in burnout.

If we are feeling burned-out, we need to take ownership to preserve our investments to date. We can't let intervening factors control us – and, as leaders, we can't let intervening factors cause burnout of employees, especially those who we consider top talent who drive our success. We need to clear paths to allow for their commitment and ability to excel. Initially, however, we may need to take action to clear a path for ourselves.

Perspectives from Experience

I was motivated to succeed during the early portion of my career. I wanted to learn how to solve problems, design solutions, and learn to lead. I wanted to excel. The initial check mark of becoming a professional engineer was replaced with becoming a lead project engineer. That was then eclipsed by becoming a project manager, followed by a team leader. Within seven years, I was an owner. Initially a junior shareholder... yes, but still an owner. Next step: vice president, major owner, and member of the Board of Directors. Check. Check. And check... all three within three years at age 32. I was committed. I had worked very hard, I routinely did things others were not willing to do in order to excel, and I didn't confuse effort with results. Through those early year efforts, I achieved a position and a level of financial reward that made me feel good and made me feel confident. It was about a year later that I began to feel a change. It was an inkling at first that my career focus was beginning to take a toll, that things were out of balance, and that my commitments and energies were not aligned with what I ultimately wanted... and needed.

21

My commitment, ownership, and drive for excellence were my assets at work, but burnout and disengagement began to slowly erode them.

The Burnout-Disengagement Cycle

When every season is a harvest season, when expectations for results only escalate, when your "all" is *always* being asked for, burnout is a real possibility. How much can we really take, especially when it seems to be continuously expected? The standard seems to have shifted. The norm is not normal... or sustainable. Trying to sustain an unsustainable pace for too long can lead to burnout.

Merriam-Webster defines burnout as: "exhaustion of physical or emotional strength or motivation usually as a result of prolonged stress or frustration." This definition doesn't seem as extreme a diagnosis as it once did. Unfortunately, it probably describes the state of most of us today.

Burnout has been on the increase and quickly moving beyond becoming a major threat to becoming an epidemic, not just to individuals experiencing it but also to organizations that employ them. Even entire industries can be victims of burnout when some of their primary occupations are routinely associated with high burnout rates, including those of physicians, nurses, educators, attorneys, and finance, including accountants. A recent study found 95 percent of human resource leaders across a variety of industries admit employee burnout is sabotaging workplace retention (Kronos Incorporated and Future Workplace, 2017; reference 1 [see References & Resources for citations]).

Stress in the workplace is a reality of life for most professionals – those who are highly skilled and perform important functions for society at large. The professional workplace has standards, practices, and procedures that must be followed. There are also times when problem solving, creativity, and guts may need to be skillfully applied in order to produce the results that we are expected, and even obligated, to produce. It is part of the reason there are relatively few of us... and why we can earn a good living – a good living that entails more than salary.

Although stress can be a routine part of the nature of our jobs, it becomes problematic if the work environment is not managed well. Today, professionals are working harder than ever. This can lead to periods of prolonged stress. The source of stress may not be the work itself, as we are trained and skilled in the work and performing it can actually give us the energy, focus, and stamina necessary to achieve results. Instead, the source of problematic stress is often the *workload*, workflow, and the work environment.

Workloads have increased for virtually all professionals across the board. Maybe the increase is due to disruptive forces in our industry. Maybe commoditization trends reduce our billings. Maybe it's the escalating costs necessary to attract employees into our organizations and to retain our talent. Maybe it's leaders who have lost touch with the realities of work and life today.

The net result is increased pressure to do more with less.

The problem for many of us is that having to "do more with less" has become more of a constant, not a temporary, situation. An easy answer is to hire additional staff, develop the full capabilities of the teams throughout the organization, and optimize workload and workflow. However, this answer is often merely a dream. The urgent realities of business today are consuming. The problem organizationally is that constant response to the urgent too often prohibits addressing the important. Creating systems and a culture that can better manage workloads and its related stress is critical.

The work environment is also problematic today. We are often required to multi-task and routinely have fragmented days filled with meetings and email. This leads to stress and even reduced efficiency. What is critical to professional and entrepreneurial performance and reduced workplace stress, and what we've lost in the busy work environment today, is time to concentrate, contemplate, plan, or even decompress after an important or stressful work event. The drive

> *We need to move beyond the urgent in order to address what's important.*

now for even more teamwork and collaboration in the workplace, if not managed well, can actually worsen the work environment for professionals who need routine time for concentration, contemplation, planning, and decompression in order to perform productively and effectively at a high level.

If workloads and the work environment are not managed well, the prolonged overload we encounter leads to overwhelm. Overwhelm can be masked for a while. Being overloaded can feel different day-to-day, project-to-project, account-to-account, case-to-case, patient-to-patient, new position-to-new position, but it is persistent and oppressive. Over time, overload turns into overwhelm. It is when overwhelm sets in that we begin to experience the physical, mental, and emotional exhaustion that leads to burnout.

HOW PROLONGED WORK OVERLOAD LEADS TO BURNOUT

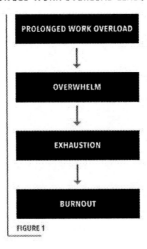

Figure 1 illustrates the steps to burnout.

Under these conditions, disengagement at work also comes into play. Disengagement is a reaction to protect ourselves, our attempt to separate us from the source of our stress and overwhelm. Merriam-Webster defines disengagement as: "to release or detach oneself: withdraw."

The most recent Gallup State of the American Workplace report (reference 2) concluded that 67 percent of U.S. employees were not engaged at work. That is two out of every three employees! Whereas 51 percent were characterized as not engaged, 16 percent were characterized as actively disengaged.

Burnout and disengagement don't happen overnight. They can take years to take root. Burnout and the isolating nature of disengagement can also form a cycle. In this way, burnout and disengagement often reinforce each other. The net result is typically a downward spiral. For the individual, this negative looping disintegrates toward a pivot away from a team, division, organization, or even an industry. Pivoting away can become the only way to break the cycle to either cope with the realities of the situation or to proactively change our environment.

THE BURNOUT-DISENGAGEMENT CYCLE AND PIVOT

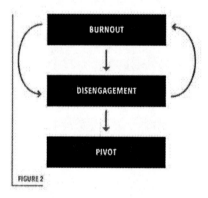

FIGURE 2

When the cycle repeats, pivoting may be the only way to break out of it.

For the teams, divisions, organizations, and industries impacted, this downward spiral and pivot is never beneficial. Highly skilled and once motivated employees, and even leaders, pivot away. The cost to replace them and the cost of the loss of their future productivity can be enormous – up to or greater than twice the salary of a senior or highly trained employee. In addition, deadlines are often missed, workloads on others further increase, and clients, patients and future referrals can be lost or poached. But, wait… there's more. A person stuck in the burnout-disengagement cycle can either directly or indirectly negatively impact others and degrade your overall culture along the way. Whether they leave due to their choice to pivot or remain in the cycle, the result for the organization is never positive.

Even when leaders aspire and work toward achieving "the dream" of hiring the necessary number of employees with the right skills and developing them to optimize workload and workflow, the reality for much of professional services is inconsistent staffing. Even in the most proactive and effectively led organizations, there are bound to be periods of time with back-to-back critical deadlines, the need to string a couple good quarters together, or get through the year successfully with less than the ideal number and composition of staff. To survive these "seasons of overload," leaders need to rely on the organization's mission, reward systems, and the intrinsic motivations and goodwill of employees.

> *Employee goodwill and aligned motivations are needed to withstand seasons of overload.*

A reality that we face today – whether due to overload or just our overall busyness – is that we lose track of things. We lose touch. We lose clarity of where we stand and how or if what we are doing fits into the "big picture."

This can often manifest itself in a loss of efficacy – feeling like we no longer have the power to produce an effect or that our efforts aren't really making a difference.

As leaders, we often stop talking about our organization's mission and vision and the future. Continual communication about our mission and vision and what the future could hold is essential for keeping busy talent on track and inspired. Organizationally we also need to connect "where the rubber hits the road." Disconnection can occur if we have outdated, ineffective, or counterproductive incentive systems. These systems don't motivate or reinforce continuous commitment to meeting or exceeding organizational needs. At the same time, intrinsic motivations of employees change over time. Most of us evolve and mature as we enter different work and life seasons. What motivated me at age 25 was not the same as what motivated me at 35 or 45. Our goodwill is also often consumed with seemingly continual near-term needs and initiatives that compound overload. This coupled with strained or non-existent relationships can leave us feeling like we are being taken advantage of. When this happens, burnout and disengagement take on a new dimension – one that adds the element of *frustration*.

Work-related frustration coupled with prolonged work overload-related burnout intensifies the burnout-disengagement cycle. It is essential for both individuals and leaders to understand and address this added dimension of work frustration if they want to reverse (and prevent) burnout and halt the burnout-disengagement cycle.

THE ADDITION OF WORK FRUSTRATION TO THE
BURNOUT-DISENGAGEMENT CYCLE

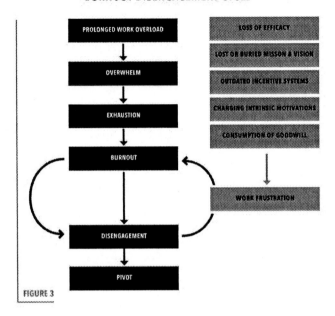

FIGURE 3

Work frustration adds another element to the burnout-disengagement cycle and professionals are a very susceptible population for this complicating factor.

Professionals are particularly susceptible to work-related frustration because we are achievers by nature. We want to do, build, serve, and have impact. We have committed and invested a lot to be where we are, and when we can't see results, when our progress is slowed or stopped, when we are experiencing a lack of control, and when we are feeling like we're missing out, we get frustrated.

If the frustrations we are dealing with today are not understood and effectively addressed, the burnout-disengagement cycle can be further fueled by resentment.

Work overload issues impact our personal lives. When we miss too much time with our family, time with our friends, and time by ourselves, it is personally frustrating. But when it is incessant and as a direct result of unaddressed work issues, that personal frustration often manifests into resentment.

This resentment can be toward leaders who choose not to see work overload and environment issues and myopically focus on the organization and near-term goals; leaders who see overload issues and give them lip service, but ultimately do nothing about them while still expecting results; or leaders who talk specifically about employees being our "biggest" or "most valuable" asset but reinforce outdated systems that perpetuate the problems. This form of "double-speak" – saying the right things but incentivizing the status quo – not only breeds resentment, it also undermines trust and confidence in leaders and organizations, and helps to validate an employee's disengagement.

THE ADDITION OF PERSONAL FRUSTRATION AND RESENTMENT TO THE BURNOUT-DISENGAGEMENT CYCLE

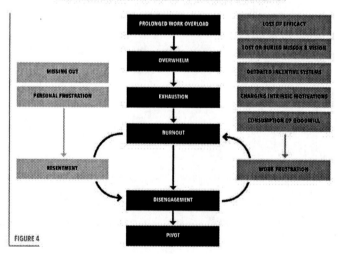

Failure to live up to employees as "the most valuable asset" increase personal frustration and resentment.

Perspectives from Experience

As a professional engineer, physical exhaustion didn't lead to frustration. I could generally deal with physical exhaustion by actually taking a weekend off from time to time, sleeping in, and having a couple of relaxed afternoons. It was even better if it was a long weekend when we didn't have things to do or places to be. Vacations improved with time. A week's vacation away was not as beneficial as a long weekend at home with little to do. Two weeks' vacation that included some time at home toward the end was better for me than two full weeks away. Of course, like many professionals, I was almost 20 years into my career before I ever took an actual two-week vacation or used all my vacation time in a given year.

Mental exhaustion became an issue. I began to recognize it in 2004, a year or so after I had become a vice president, practice group leader, and joined the Board of Directors. I was 33 and was beginning to recognize some of the downsides to being admittedly a workaholic. Like many, I gradually internalized the needs of work as my personal needs. I was constantly thinking of work, and this one-way relationship led

> **Internalizing "work" needs as "personal" needs and allowing too much of your identity to be defined by career leads to burnout.**

to work becoming my identity. Needing to continuously perform and grow the business as a measure of who I was as a person became exhausting. There was little to no separation between me and my work. There was no time for

31

consistent physical activity for either better health or stress relief, but I knew I did need some relief.

I can't quite remember the specific motivation to act, but I remember at that time being drawn to a service trip that was being offered through my church to a location in the developing world. Maybe I liked the idea of an escape. Maybe I liked the challenge of something new. Maybe I just knew something was off or missing. Whatever contributed to my attraction, I will forever be grateful for the opportunity. That trip in '05 was what I would later term my "timeout." That trip also began what I later termed my "parallel life."

The travel and the work on this eight-day trip were physically tiring but the wider perspective on life was mentally and emotionally invigorating – at least temporarily. The new experience and the personal growth afforded me months of working without mental exhaustion. However, the pull of the work demands to which I returned eventually took over my mental energy and pushed aside any continued personal and emotional growth. This see-saw of going away each year to serve and be invigorated followed by the resurfacing of work-related mental exhaustion and postponement of personal and emotional growth continued for a few years.

For much of my early career, my "present" was a calculated investment in providing for myself, my family, and my future. In contrast to work at that time, serving others gave much more than it took. I experienced the truth that it is better to give than to receive. Serving provided a much needed broader perspective on life, and it shed new light on the value of others and community. Serving *connected me with greater meaning and purpose. Serving also sparked new interests, curiosities, and growth. As my parallel life progressed, not only was I looking for more than temporary relief for work that was otherwise consuming, I wanted to make more of an impact, and I wanted to share that with others.*

2009 was a pivotal year for me. Three separate things were intersecting at this time. First, on a personal level, I was continuing to grow in self- and social-awareness. I had a new and expanded world view. My family life improved as we participated together in the service work, and I was living up to my personal vow to actually use my vacation time and not to miss any more of my kids' high school years other than what was absolutely necessary.

At this time, I was continuing to excel at work, and as a leader, I was improving. I knew that this was all in direct proportion to my personal growth and better balance – and that I would not be reverting to my previous state of mind. I also knew that I had exercised the power of my leadership position to rescript the life I wanted to now have.

Looking back, a "fade" also began at this time. It was a fade in my interest in work. The fade grew in proportion to a lack of inspiration and a growing frustration about the future. The fade matured over time to become the

> **A sense of connectedness and serving others is a foundational human need.**

pivot. I didn't dislike the work we were doing, but the projects and the victories no longer meant as much to me. I

33

knew the work. I knew how to win. I knew how to be profitable. But I began to question the purpose. Winning at work was clearly more of a milestone for me than the destination to which I had mentally committed to early on. I also began to question the pace and question the expectations to continually over-achieve. I began to see the impact the long hours every week, every month, and every year were having on our staff – especially our key staff. I shifted from a project-centric focus to a people- and organization-centric interest. I became frustrated at what I perceived as double-speak related to operational matters affecting our "most valuable assets" that I saw as short term and short sighted. I was becoming convinced that necessary changes to the status quo may be a mirage – and I began to resent the possible presence of a mirage.

The third thing that was happening was a drive for impact and a desire for more connection. The resistance to change at work led me to invest more in service to others. And these doors were wide open. In 2009, with my confidence in serving others growing, I was presented with an opportunity to leverage routine work skills in a new context. That summer, our family decided to vacation at a child refuge center at which we had been serving as part of my parallel life. There was chronic flooding that now threatened to undermine the children's feeding center. Erosion from heavy rains had rapidly carved a new and much wider chasm, and that opening in the earth was now within a foot of the building's foundation. Immediately, I brainstormed possible fixes using materials that were readily available on the rural island with the center's director and one of her contacts. With a small notepad and pen, a fix was designed – and it worked. Professionally speaking, this was a pretty minor effort. Personally speaking, however, this was a major breakthrough. With this opportunity, I realized that I had skills that could really help others, that I could help solve problems, and that I could actually have an impact, and not just as part of a team.

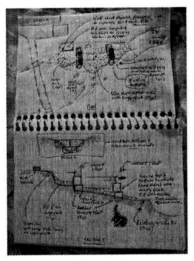

It was empowering and over the next several years, I helped lead the design of multiple erosion control, roadway, water, and building projects for the refuge center; the development of a university earning program for talented and motivated teens; and later a social enterprise farm business to help fund the refuge center and university program, and to provide local jobs. I was also co-leading a growing number of service teams to the refuge center and local community to build and further develop the projects. Seeing the great need for skills and experiencing the power of sharing these skills in a new

context, we routinely engaged other professionals including engineers, architects, attorneys, doctors, nurses, teachers, graphic designers, builders, accountants, and financial folks on the projects.

Two years later, as we were working through our firm's strategic and succession planning sessions, I knew I was at a fork in the road. I was unwilling to "go back" to where I was before my '05 timeout. I continued to be frustrated with the status quo. At the same time, I was still

drawn to the growth and impact embedded with serving. At this moment, I was asking myself some bigger questions: Could I affect enough change fast enough at work to keep me interested and motivated? Could I leave and do something different? What would I do? How much would that pay? What would my wife say? Were things really that bad? How could I unwind the deeply intertwined position I held? Would I have the courage to break from my past and commit to a future that was more aligned with what I wanted?

The Alternatives

Organizations can and do function with burned-out and disengaged employees. Depending on a variety of factors, organizational leaders could embrace the realities of operating with burned-out and disengaged employees as an acceptable cost of doing business. That is clearly a decision for organizational leaders to make. It's not a very wise decision, and if organizational leaders don't take action to address burnout and disengagement, individuals have options, too.

Staying in the Organization:

Employees can choose to stay with an organization and deal with the burnout and disengagement. They can remain quiet about their feelings or they can be more publicly vocal. Either way, employees who are burned-out and disengaged – especially those actively disengaged – are likely to create some collateral damage via disengaging other employees, negatively impacting the culture, and lowering the standards of excellence in most organizations. Even if the money is good and staying will help you achieve admirable goals such as helping your kid through college, paying off your mortgage, or saving enough to get that vacation home you would like to retire to one day, staying in the organization is likely to create collateral damage to you as well.

First, there are negative health and relationship consequences to continually operating in the environments of burnout and disengagement. If staying results in us being chronically unhappy, that can lead to relationship strains and even lead to depression. Staying under worsening conditions could also lead to a health incident. Any of these consequences are likely to negatively impact both you and those you are trying to help by staying.

Second, staying too long could lead to a more emotionally charged exit when that day arrives. Reaching a point of being totally fed-up or "not being able to take it anymore" is more likely to result in burned bridges that can negatively impact your next position or venture.

Finally, you could be let go or fired for a lack of productivity. Burnout and disengagement can contribute to "presenteeism," or being present but not motivated, focused, or productive at work. Presenteeism is a major cost to employers that has gotten more attention. Recent studies report that, on average, employees operate at 75 percent of their capacity as a result of coming to work either physically or mentally unwell, costing businesses the equivalent of three months per year in lost productivity

> *A burned-out, disengaged employee is costly to any organization and often negatively impacts others and the corporate culture.*

(Global Corporate Challenge, 2016; reference 3). It is hard to mask your lack of motivation and whatever else may result from burnout and disengagement for long, especially if you are frustrated and have grown resentful. In this case, the organization makes a decision *for you*, and that decision will likely more significantly set back your efforts for a smooth transition to your next position or venture.

Other options for staying in your organization despite the presence of burnout and disengagement can include: developing a "side-hustle," remaining full-time but cutting back, or switching to part-time.

Perspectives from Experience

As I was transitioning out of my career in engineering, I tried each of these alternatives before eventually pivoting away. During my initial burnout-disengagement cycle, I voiced my opinions in attempt to change the status quo. Later, I grew mostly silent and worked on attaining financial goals that would better position me for a possible next venture. That worked for a few years, as I was fully engaged and growing in my side-hustle and able push my "personal status quo." My side-hustle was not a secondary job or source of income; it was the parallel life I described earlier. At some point, however, I knew a change was inevitable. My time, energy, and future life became worth more to me than the money. I needed more time to plan that change. I still committed to my job and even enjoyed aspects related to strategic planning and business and staff development, but something needed to give. I decided that that something would be my "second 40," or the routine work hours over

40 each week. No more work on the weekends or at night – that would be the time I would devote to figuring out exactly what my next venture would be.

That strategy did not work for long. There were too many expectations from others. When external pressures to devote more time from my "second 40" moved from awkward and uncomfortable to unhealthy levels, I made the permanent decision to pivot toward my future. It was then that I negotiated my departure.

As part of the agreement, I would work six months full-time with "reset" expectations, and then transition to part-time. There were plenty of challenges in those last months. Maybe it was the unique nature of this situation or the general newness of professionals choosing to transition for non-retirement reasons, but some of the awkwardness and discomfort continued. In addition, some of the more strategic initiatives I was interested in pursuing during this transition were not of interest to others, so I decided to have a limited part-time season and accelerate my plans to pivot away.

Pivoting Away from the Organization:

Employees who decide that they can no longer tolerate the burnout and disengagement may choose to pivot away. Options for pivoting away from an organization can include: conventional retirement, retirement to an encore career, leaving the organization for a competitor, leaving the organization and venturing out on your own, and leaving both the organization and the industry.

ALTERNATIVES TO THE BURNOUT-DISENGAGEMENT CYCLE

	HELPS ADDRESS BURNOUT	PROVIDES OPPORTUNITY FOR ENGAGEMENT
STAY IN THE ORGANIZATION		
Remain full time, develop a side hustle		✓
Remain full time, but cut back	✓	
Go part time	✓	
PIVOT AWAY FROM ORGANIZATION		
Conventional retirement	✓	✓
Retire to an encore career	✓	✓
Leave organization & go to competition	✓	✓
Leave organization & go out on own	✓	✓
Leave both organization & industry	✓	✓

FIGURE 5

Figure 5 summarizes each of the options described.

As you can see from the graphic, short of an organization addressing burnout and disengagement, all of the individual options for addressing burnout result in less focus, less time or no time in the organization. Individual options obviously focus on the employee and what is best for them. There are huge costs to replacing talent that leaves an organization. As presented, replacement costs can be up to or greater than twice the salary of a senior or highly trained employee.

These higher costs associated with employee loss and turnover are particularly true in professional services. In addition to the direct replacement costs, there are other costs associated with lost productivity in the organization and the lost future value of their contacts and influence. All of these costs further support the significant return on investment organizations can realize by investing to retain employees by reducing and eliminating burnout and disengagement, especially in top and senior talent.

On the other hand, for individuals, there has never been a better time to pivot away from organizations that allow burnout and disengagement to occur and fester. Part-time and post-retirement volunteering is being marketed and filling a major need for people in the second half of their adult lives to connect with others and their communities after a near full focus on a singular industry or engaging primarily in generating a positive bottom line. Encore careers in both the nonprofit and for-profit spaces are in vogue. The freelance or "gig" economy is strong and growing and is encouraging and supporting side-hustles. Entrepreneurship is booming, and tools to help both the serious and more hobby-minded entrepreneurs are pretty much everywhere these days. This is in addition to costs and barriers of entry into markets being lower now than they have ever been in history, thanks to democratization of technology, the internet, and social media.

> *There has never been an easier time than now for employees to pivot away from an organization.*

This all being said, there is a "tragic" element in the fact that professionals in many cases are being forced to pivot away from organizations or careers because of burnout and disengagement. These are smart, motivated, and talented people who have committed years to master their craft and often wired to achieve... now choosing to do something different or leave practices just to cope with the effects of burnout and disengagement. What does this say about our society, our industries, and our organizations?

There is also a tragic element for organizations. Notwithstanding the high costs of having burned-out and disengaged employees, the most talented employees are often the most mobile. Your most talented employees are most likely to pivot away. It is also getting harder for less-than-great organizations to attract top

> *Burnout and disengagement is growing rampant in most professional services fields, and industries – like organizations – will need to become much more attractive to entice and retain top talent.*

talent to either replace lost talent or grow. Today, the news of the departure of a professional spreads immediately. There are also many websites at which employees can post their reviews of your organization. It is more important than ever that organizations become attractive workplaces and workplace destinations in order thrive or, in some cases, even to survive.

The same holds true for some industries. Burnout and disengagement is growing or rampant in most professional services fields. This is especially true in medical, legal, education, and financial services.

There is a better way. There is an answer. Careers, organizations, and industries need to engage in a refresh.

We will need to pause, develop a new approach, and hit a reset button.

Key Points

- It takes commitment and ownership to excel as a professional and a business owner today, but neither commitment nor ownership in the pursuit of excelling at our craft alone causes burnout.
- Excelling at our craft is a key driver and positive motivator for professionals and business owners. Excelling is also expected from our clients, customers, and patients.
- Burnout and disengagement is real and erodes our motivation, commitment to our craft, and ability to perform. Burnout and disengagement only create loss for individuals, organizations, and even industries.
- Leadership needs to make addressing burnout and disengagement a real priority, not a competing priority, if it is to be solved.
- For leaders and organizations that don't credibly and effectively take action to address burnout and disengagement, there is no better time than now for individuals to develop a side-hustle or pivot away to a new venture – not to mention being a great demand for their services from competing organizations as part of the "talent war."

Chapter Two:

The Losing Side of Busy

As I presented at the start of this section, burnout, disengagement, and feeling trapped are problematic symptoms of larger issues. In addition to the problems of prolonged work overload, unaddressed frustration, and the loss of inspiration and motivation I presented in Chapter 1, many of us are dealing with problems arising from the fact that we are losing touch, losing track, and losing clarity in our lives.

All our busyness only adds to this "loss." The consuming nature of our overall busyness often stops us from taking advantage of opportunities that may benefit us and our organizations that would ultimately help reverse some of the problems associated with burnout. The demands of today are seemingly too urgent and pressing, and many of us remain in a fog. In order to live the life we desire, we need to be intentional about our actions. A lack of action to begin to win again is a decision to continue with the status quo.

Losing Touch

Despite all of our increased connections through smart phones, alerts, instant messages, and the many forms of social media, we are actually becoming more *disconnected* today, and as a result, our ability to lead effective lives and organizations is impacted.

Because we are so busy, we often don't see it happening. We're actually too busy to take a minute to look up and around and take note of it. Only when we consciously look to address reconnecting do we do so. That is unless or until we have an intervening event, such as an illness or an accident or have a series of negative experiences that force us to pause and take notice. This phenomenon of lost connections that plagues us today can be best explained through the concept of emotional intelligence.

The concept of emotional intelligence has been popularized by several, including Daniel Goleman and Travis Bradberry. The data about emotional intelligence is clear. Emotionally intelligent people are more successful at work and at life and are better leaders. Emotional intelligence is what draws people (i.e., our friends, colleagues, employees, clients, customers, patients, and students, etc.) to like, know, and trust us. Emotionally intelligent people attract and inspire others up and down the corporate ladder, on the front line, and in the back office. Interactions with emotionally intelligent people are more relational and less transactional – which makes them so much more effective.

Emotional intelligence is different from the intelligence measured as the "IQ" (intelligence quotient) we are born with and helps explain why people with average IQs outperform people with the highest IQs 70 percent of the time and why 90 percent of top performers have high levels of emotional intelligence (Drs. Travis Bradberry and Jean Greaves, *Emotional Intelligence 2.0;* reference 4). Emotional intelligence, measured as "EQ" (emotional quotient), is a measure of our self-awareness, self-management, social-awareness, and our relationship management. Having high levels of EQ would include understanding and being able to appropriately control and leverage our emotions, knowing our strengths and weaknesses, understanding what drives us in terms of values, motivations and goals, understanding how our actions and attitudes impact ourselves and others, having empathy for others, being able to consider others when making decisions, and being able to appropriately and effectively communicate with others.

Our emotional intelligence can be increased over time. Emotional intelligence can also be *lost* over time. The problem we, as individuals and organizational leaders, need to recognize is that, on average, professionals and high achievers actually *lose* emotional intelligence as we become increasingly successful in our careers. It was the very graphic (Figure 6) that was the turning point for me that I shared at the start of this book. It instantly articulated exactly what had happened to me.

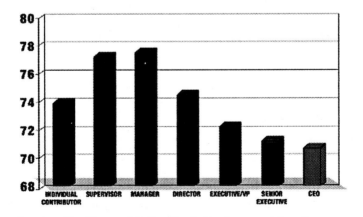

Emotional Intelligence 2.0, Drs. Travis Bradberry and Jean Greaves

Perspectives from Experience

As I had achieved and became more successful in my career, I became less self-aware outside of my work goals and less socially aware outside of work... that is until I called my timeout in 2005. The demands of the work to this point resulted in the loss of connections with myself and others although I worked hard not to lose connections with my immediate family. The connections I lost were with more extended family and those with friends and neighbors. Those relationships were always on a "fit in if there is space" basis, if at all, during the first half of my career. It wasn't by design. I was simply too busy and too focused at the time to even notice it.

What immediately resonated with me about this graphic was that it validated the losses I began to feel as my career advanced through its first half. The loss was losing touch with who I was and knowing whether I was still on the right path. The loss was in being able to answer some of the bigger questions I had as I progressed in life:

> **Beware the loss of emotional intelligence. You're likely to lose it when you need it most.**

What did I want and what did I want to stand for? Would maintaining my position at work contribute to achieving all my goals or make it harder? The loss was also in the quality of relationships with others – both inside and outside of work.

As we make our name and build our careers, we often don't have time for many relationships outside of the office. Inside the office, we are also often hampered in establishing meaningful relationships. If and as we proceed up the corporate ladder, our position and competition often intervenes to maintain distances. For many of us, we have colleagues, peers, subordinates, and supervisors at work – not close friends. This can be especially true for leaders and managers. Despite position, it is lonely at or near the top for many leaders. This separation takes a toll on us. This separation can also limit the number of trusted people we know who can challenge us, grow us, hold us accountable, and keep us on track. It's an unlikely Catch-22: The more we need others as we succeed the more distant and isolated we become.

With the compelling data before me in that graphic, I immediately knew that the rebuilding and expansion of my self- and social-awareness and my ability to manage both emanated from my parallel life. The personal growth that had resulted from those experiences was what made me a better leader at work and a better person in life.

The data proved that I was not alone. High achievers on average are losing emotional intelligence. Dozens of professionals and business owners I know continue to reveal that they feel and experience these losses. Armed with this concept and data, they almost universally better understand that internal whisper for more awareness and connection – and why they are also longing for greater meaning and purpose and a much fuller and balanced life.

Following my timeout and as I progressed along my parallel life, I knew firsthand the organizational value that could be gained in creating environments for employees to build back lost emotional intelligence. I thought this to be especially true for our highest achievers and high-potentials who were burning out and becoming disengaged. I saw this as both a way to provide something that was missing for employees, contributing to their growing frustrations, and as a way to grow the business through renewed individual motivation and organizational engagement. I wanted the result that organizations with higher levels of emotional intelligence enjoy. However, at the time of our 2011 strategic and succession planning and until my final paycheck, I only grew more frustrated with the continued stagnation in what I saw as the status quo and the burnout-disengagement cycle.

There is another Catch-22 here, and we need to offer leaders a period of grace as a result. The statistics are true for all. The reality is that leaders themselves have lost or are losing their own emotional intelligence. Even when leaders decide they want to take action to restore their own EQ, they may be too busy or tied to conventional business practices to create systems to rebuild and continue to grow the emotional intelligence of employees. To rebuild and grow emotional intelligence on the job may be considered by some established leaders to be inappropriate, costly, or risky. That mindset needs to change if a leader or an organization wants to remain relevant today and thrive. The benefits of emotional intelligence for professionals and organizations that are client-, customer-, patient-, and student-facing are more than convincing.

Designing environments for employees to become more socially and self-aware as part of their job takes both an investment in time and an investment in strategy, but the return on investment can be substantial for both the individuals involved and the organization – and can be a positive start to a new season of growth.

Different Seasons, Different Goals

We have distinct work and life seasons… and they matter. We may not have been told about these seasons or we may be too busy to think about them or the opportunities and implications of having them. We may even be so busy that we haven't even realized we've transitioned from one season to the next. We may be losing track.

For the purposes of understanding more about our seasons and how they intersect, overlap, and impact our lives, I have outlined an example. This example is based on my direct experience and my learnings through dozens of leadership, self-help, and organizational development books and articles as well as dozens, if not hundreds, of related conversations, podcasts, sermons, and teachings within the past decade. Our specific life circumstances and timing of events that create our seasons will differ, but the example can be adapted to better understand our unique situations.

Work Seasons:

There are four typical "work" seasons that are understood by more established professionals and business owners. These seasons have some aspects that make them timeless truths and some aspects that are associated with more conventional thinking. The seasons are: the "mastering our craft" season; the "making a name" season;

the "making a difference" season; and the "leaving a legacy" season.

The "mastering your craft" season is when we work to become proficient in our chosen professions. We work to become licensed, registered, certified, and progress to operate in responsible charge of assignments. This learning and development season can last up to 10 years from the time we begin our careers.

The "making a name" season is when we leverage our proficiency to larger or more complex assignments and when we take on management and leadership roles through successive promotions. This season of further mastering our craft and ascending the corporate ladder can last up to another 15 years.

> *As professionals, we have work seasons, and as humans, we have life seasons.*

At about the 25-year mark, a shift can and often does occur. At this point in our careers, we have put in our time and been all in and committed for many years. We may be more established and comfortable in our organizations and in our industry and more comfortable in terms of personal finances. At this stage, for many of us, growing our careers entails shifting from a "me" focus to a "we" focus. If so, the "making a difference" season begins. This season is when we, as more established senior managers and leaders, have a better handle on our personal success drivers and motivations and see our primary roles as coaching and supporting others to help them do and be their best. We leverage our knowledge and experience to improve others' understandings and abilities to successfully accomplish goals and complete tasks. This season can last up to 15 years.

The final season is the "leaving a legacy" season. This is when our primary focus may be to share perspectives and pass along knowledge to help inspire the next generation and help perpetuate the organization and its mission. This season can last up to 10 years.

Figure 7 illustrates these work seasons along a year of experience timeline.

Life Seasons:

There are three typical "life" seasons many of us experience as adults: the pre-family "me" season; the "family" season; and the post-family "empty-nest" season.

The "me" season can be a "we" season if we're married and don't yet have children. For the purposes of this example, we can assume that the "me" (or "we") season can last up to 10 years from the time we leave school. The "family" season can last 20 years and can be subdivided to include the "raising" phase, say 15 years, and the later "letting go" phase, say five years. The "empty-nest" season can last up to 20 years and can be subdivided to include the "pre-grandchildren" phase, say 10 years, and the "grandchildren" phase, say 10 years.

Figure 8 illustrates these life seasons along the same timeline as the work seasons and with the assumption that we left school and began our career at age 22.

When I first took the time to layout and try to align my work and life seasons, I found it pretty fascinating. In this example, and as part of my own life mapping, the following items are often found:

1. We can have an active adult work-life timeline of up to 50 years.
2. Our work and life seasons do not always align.
3. Transitioning from our "master our craft" season to our "make a name" season at work can coincide with transitioning from our "me/we" season to our "family" season in life. This shift makes sense in that we would now be working to provide for our family's financial needs.
4. Transitioning from our "make a name" season to our "make a difference" season at work can coincide with our transition from our family

season's "raising" phase to the "letting go" phase. This shift again makes sense as, at this point, we may be operating at fairly high levels of expertise at work and looking for more challenges. Depending on our circumstances, it may be harder to find those challenges at work. We may also be in a comfortable financial position and the allure of money may not be the same as it once was. This could be especially true if, at the time, it became apparent to us that our kids were suddenly growing up and time with them is growing short. In this context, many of us become retrospective and wonder what life will be like in the future when the kids leave to begin their own lives. Aligned with our shift at work, our interests and actions often shift to more of a coach and supporter role. Our goal becomes to pour into our kids as much of our wisdom and knowledge as possible so that they can be prepared and be their best and work to maximize our positive impact.

5. Similarly, transitioning from our "make a difference" season to our "leave a legacy" season at work can coincide with our transition from our empty-nest season's "pre-grandchildren" phase to the "grandchildren" phase. This can make sense as we may be beginning to face our mortality and want to give back as much as possible to those who will follow in our footsteps.

Each of our work and life seasons is different and comes with different goals and aspirations. These changes are reflective of where we are in life and the experiences we have had to date. Each season can also represent a transition point or "fork in the road" that we need to navigate.

There can be conflict and confusion if we don't navigate well from one season to the next or we are not operating in sync with our present season. For example, if we have a family and operate in "me" season mode, there can be conflict and confusion. Similarly, if we operate in a family "raising" phase mode when our family is really in the "letting go" phase, we can also have conflict and confusion.

Understanding both life and work seasons will help you avoid the conflict and confusion that often occurs at their transition points.

On the work front, if we have mastered our craft and new opportunities to leverage our proficiency to larger and more complex assignments or opportunities for greater management and leadership roles don't come our way, it can be frustrating. Similarly, when we are no longer inspired and motivated by aspects of our jobs, and no new growth opportunities are available, we could grow both bored and frustrated.

Transitions between work seasons can affect our non-work life, and transitions between life seasons can affect our work. As presented in some of the observations listed above, these transitions between seasons and phases can complement each other. Transitions between seasons and phases can also work against each other and contribute to feeling burned-out, bored, and trapped.

Perspectives from Experience

Starting our family on the early side, I didn't have much of a "me" or "we" season. As a result, I did all that I could to shorten my "master our craft" season and push into "making a name" as early as I could. Fortunately, I had a series of tremendous managers and mentors, and the great start to my career in Boston set me up for a rapid ascent in Maine. Although about a decade ahead of the example's timeline, the sequence of my shifting from the "making a name" to the "making a difference" season was similar to that of the example coinciding with our family season shift from the "raising" to the "letting go" phase. From my perspective as an individual, these transitions between my work and life seasons were complementary.

Whether it was because I was ahead of a more typical life season timeline or due to a very strong performance-based work culture, there was some conflict and confusion as I was looking to make the transition from "making a name" to "making a difference" at work.

Initially there was some support and encouragement for my parallel life at work. For some, it was a curiosity, and for some, it was a marketing opportunity. A number of service-minded peers also contributed to designs and some even helped build projects. I was also allowed to use available equipment to support some of the work. This was beneficial and it was part of what helped extend my mental benefits of the annual trip experience from eight days to months afterward.

The conflict and confusion started about halfway through my transition process after I had concluded that the business would not be willing to contribute enough as a partner to my "making a difference" season. That conclusion was drawn during that strategic and succession planning period in 2011. The primary culprit was burnout. With my vow a couple of years earlier to take all my vacation time and spend more time with my family, I was feeling less burned-out than in the past. Just having more control to make decisions can alleviate burnout. In this case, I was the boss and could take control to make decisions that worked best to accommodate my goals. I went further to count the possible cost: 10 hours was about 15 to 20 percent of my near constant 50- to 60-hour workweek. During that season, those 10 hours per week were worth much more to me than 15 to 20 percent of my bonus. Other employees, even top employees, didn't have or feel the freedom I had to make that decision – and that added to my frustrations.

The work environment itself had many great qualities – smart, talented, motivated, and committed people. Customer service and technical excellence united our culture. It was a great place to grow technically and be part of a successful and high-performing organization. With so much success, many seemed confused about my concerns related to the more widespread burnout and disengagement I saw surfacing. I wanted to explore this further and make adjustments. I was interested as an individual who experienced and was still trying to work through the burnout-disengagement cycle. I was interested as a more emotionally connected and empathetic leader. I was also interested as a major owner in the firm. I needed to ensure my investment was both safe and poised to grow. As the youngest major owner and member of the Board, and with seemingly the longest tenure left, I needed to ensure our performance would be sustainable and be able to be further expanded well into the future. My visions of just how to ensure this were often in conflict with prevailing views.

As an individual, I was also in conflict with having to live parallel lives. I had successfully integrated my work skills into my service life, but there was no opening to integrate my service skills into my career or my firm. This added to my frustration at the time.

Generations in the Workplace

Although there are certainly some distinctions between generations in the workplace today, much of the distinction seems more related to our different seasons than our generations. That said, today there is

> *Today, creating impact in the workplace can unite across generations, offices, teams, departments, divisions, positions, and tenure.*

greater cross-generational convergence related to one aspect that top leaders are beginning to better understand and leverage. This convergence is related to impact. Today, most of us want to have a greater impact. We want to have a direct effect on creating something positive, or we want to be part of a team that creates that positive or allows that positive to grow. Whether it be a seasonal shift to make more of a difference or give back, or be part of a growing desire to live a more integrated life, having an impact at work can also be a unifying element across offices, teams, departments, divisions, positions, and tenure.

In general, millennials desire to have impact in life and are also looking to have it integrated as part of their work and careers. They are looking to do and to participate in governance, environmental, or socially related matters that go beyond conventional business. The focus of the desired impact can change from season to season, but the goal on the work front at least will be to help effect something positive beyond "business as usual" or "business for business sake."

Having this type of impact was typically not on the mind of baby boomers as they entered and progressed through their careers. Life and work was mostly compartmentalized. However, the desire for this separation is changing. Having spent years, if not decades, dedicated to their careers, greater numbers of boomers are looking to volunteer more and have a growing interest in engaging in their communities more on the job through corporate social impact initiatives. This makes sense in terms of work and life seasons, too. Boomers are now in the "make a difference" and "leave a legacy" work seasons and likely have more time and more seasoned perspectives now with many also simultaneously in the "empty-nest" life season.

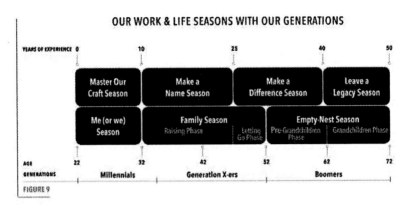

OUR WORK & LIFE SEASONS WITH OUR GENERATIONS

Figure 9 adds the component of the current workplace generations to the work-life season graphics.

Generation Xers are generally more philosophically aligned with the millennials in their desire to have an impact in life and be able to make a difference at work in ways beyond business as usual. Many Generation Xers are making the shift from the "make a name" to the "make a difference" season at work and shifting from the family "raising" phase to the family "letting go" phase in life. These transitions for many are helping to provide more inspiration to consider and pursue life and career adjustments. Gen Xers are also beginning to take on more leadership roles in organizations that can help facilitate desired adjustments.

Gen Xers are the bridge between the larger boomer and millennial generations. Given their philosophical leanings, their work and life season shifts, and the interests of the millennials behind them, work environments under the leadership of Gen Xers are poised for change. However, present leaders need to take note: Having been forced to come to age work-wise with major recessions in the early 1990s, early 2000s, and another beginning in 2008, and needing to conform more to the ideals of the boomers to date due to their comparatively small numbers, the Gen Xers are some of the most burned-out and disengaged professionals today. If burnout and disengagement is not addressed now for many Gen Xers, they may not be around in organizations or industries to take over leadership roles... and they may not be there to help train and develop the millennials and others entering the workforce.

> *Changing work and life seasons and generational differences make addressing burnout and disengagement critical to the success of future leadership transitions.*

Keeping Score

Getting reconnected and keeping track of our seasons can better position us to address burnout, but many of us also need to re-establish our clarity. Are we on the right path? Are we on track to live the life we desire? Will this next promotion help me to have the impact I want or am destined to have?

Having clarity of where we are in life provides perspective. Having perspective can be especially important in light of a possible 50-year work-life time horizon.

Given this time horizon, many of us need to think bigger and more strategically about work and life. Doing so will help adjust our mindset, help us better see and understand how one season fits with another and how seasons can be leveraged to help move us toward the life we desire, and may help reduce some concerns or anxieties we have about the future.

We will need to be intentional in order to establish and maintain a view of our "big picture." We need to routinely make the time and invest the effort to map this out and keep it updated knowing that our lives as professionals and business owners require near continuous focus in order to establish and maintain our success.

There is a flow and pattern to life. In fact, there is a flow and a pattern that helps explain virtually all human phenomena. That flow takes the general shape of the Sigmoid Curve.

The Sigmoid or "S" Curve is in the shape of an elongated forward slanting "S." The path begins with a learning and development phase, followed by a growth phase, and then peaking and declining phases.

We follow the Sigmoid Curve as we age. Businesses often use the Sigmoid concept to better understand their product and service cycles. The goal is to know when to refresh or pivot away from one product or service to another in order to sustain growth and push into the future peaking and decline phases.

THE SIGMOID OR S-CURVE PHASES

Figure 10 depicts the typical Sigmoid Curve that indicates when it's time to pivot or refresh.

Although we can't really alter the trajectory of the curve as we age through our physical lives on earth, we can use the Sigmoid concept in terms of understanding and altering the trajectory of our careers and personal lives. Knowing where we are on our work and life curves is a key aspect to understanding where our momentum may be taking us and whether that destination is aligned with our goals and desires. The process to develop our curves is essentially scorekeeping – developing an accounting of our past to see where we stand. With this information, we can then assess whether we are on the right path or in need of a refresh or a pivot from our current trajectory.

Perspectives from Experience

Outside designing biological treatment systems as part of my engineering career, the first time I came upon another use for the Sigmoid Curve concept as an adult was when I read the book Halftime *by Bob Buford. This was one of a handful of a pivotal books that helped me navigate my life transition. The shape of the curve and the process of being committed to learning and development, energized by growth and sensing a maturing of the growth and energy, followed by peaking and decline phases was exactly how I felt about my career at that time. I was more than intrigued; I needed to map this out. At this time in 2014, my interest in work was rapidly declining.*

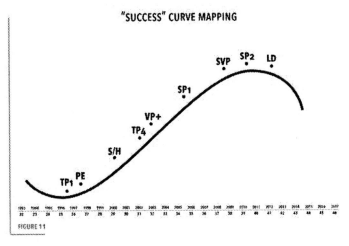

Figure 11 is what I mapped at this time and termed my "success" curve.

Since success requires commitment and commitment starts with interest, I mapped my interest in work along a timeline from when I graduated college (1993) to my then present decline (2014). I knew my interest in my career as it was had peaked between 2010 and '11 as we began a significant strategic and succession planning process. This was the second major strategic planning process I was involved with – so I marked that point (SP_2). I knew that I was pretty good and becoming proficient at "my craft" with the design of the first treatment plant around 1996 and became licensed as a professional engineer in 1998 – so I marked those points (TP_1 and P.E.). I then documented parts of my rapid accent becoming a shareholder in 2001, leading the design of my fourth treatment plant in 2002, and becoming a vice president, major owner and joining the Board of Directors in 2003 – so I marked those points (S/H, TP_4, and VP+). After a strategic planning event in 2006, I began for the first time to feel a moderated interest in work – so I marked that point (SP_1). Despite becoming a senior vice president in 2008, I was feeling more of a deceleration of my interest in work – so I marked that point (SVP). After I knew things had started to decline, I tried many other things to revive my interests. In 2012, I bought a piece of property at auction with the goal to have the zoning changed, design the subdivision, and sell or develop the parcels. That pursuit was very successful, but my interest in my career, even as a land developer on the side, was still declining – so I marked that point (LD). I then connected the dots. Amazingly to me at that time was that my career followed the shape of the S-curve. But I didn't stop there.

I was not binge-watching as I lost interest in my career. I was working as hard and as passionately as I had earlier in my career – only now that interest was directed toward my parallel life. I tried to put the S-curve concept to the test. Would it also help explain my parallel life? What I

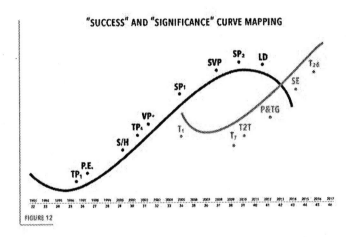

Figure 12 depicts the overlap of my career and parallel life.

mapped is included as Figure 12. This is what I termed my "significance" curve. Both the "success" and "significance" terminology I used was consistent with that of Bob Buford.

I began my "significance" curve with my timeout and first service trip in 2005 (T_1). I then marked my major service breakthrough on our family trip to the child refuge center in 2009. This was actually my seventh trip to a developing world location at that time, and since my learning and development had risen to the point where I felt I had the competence and confidence to do more – I *marked that point (T₇). That is also the time I stepped up my game in helping to co-lead our annual service trips. By 2011, I'd turned a corner. That year, our numbers had grown and we began offering two service trips and we began our university education program named Talents to Treasures, so I marked that point (T2T). Our projects and teams continued to grow and expand over the next several years, so I marked this growth period (P&TG). In 2015, we further expanded and began a social enterprise farm (SE), and by the end of the following year, I had completed 26 trips and my interest in serving others had not waned, so I marked that point (T₂₆). My "significance" curve had the makings of a similar S shape.*

I felt good about the better clarity surrounding my career and my parallel life, but I was not satisfied. I was still feeling trapped and not able to fully integrate what I wanted out of work and life. There was more work to do.

Key Points

- Despite all the new connectedness we enjoy through technology and social media, we are increasingly disconnected from meaningful relationships and isolated by our work which contributes to burnout and disengagement.
- As a result of our busyness, we are increasingly losing touch, losing track, and losing clarity in and of our lives which also contributes to burnout and disengagement.
- Ninety percent of top performers have high levels of emotional intelligence yet, on average, we lose emotional intelligence as

we climb and operate on elevated rungs of the corporate ladder. This disconnect contributes to individual burnout and disengagement and also helps explain why many leaders and organizations have been unable recognize or address burnout and disengagement in their organizations to date.

- We each have a series of seasons – both work and life seasons. How and when these overlap and intersect often dictate whether there will be conflict and confusion or whether our seasons will be more complementary.
- Changing work and life seasons and generational differences make addressing burnout and disengagement critical to the success of future leadership transitions.
- Knowing where we are on our work and life curves is a key aspect to understanding where our momentum may be taking us and whether that destination is aligned with our goals and desires.

The Losing Side of Busy

Chapter Three:

Trapped Between FOTS & FOMO

Is that where you are? Feeling trapped between FOTS – fear of the same – and FOMO – fear of missing out?

We often bear the load of busyness and the pace of burnout despite the exhaustion and despite losing touch with those around us and losing track and clarity of where we stand. This is often presented to us as the only option, and it is what we have come to know. For many of us, it can be our reality and it can also appear to be our fate. Eventually, however, there comes a point when the unsustainable can logically no longer be sustained and the cost of our losing hurts more than our winning. This is the point at which we feel a need to take action... but we can initially feel trapped.

Reaching the point of action can be sudden and unexpected. We can be presented with a health-related issue, scare, or tragedy. We can suffer a relationship issue, a separation, or a divorce. We can also be forced to deal with an unexpected work-related downturn, restructuring, merger, acquisition, or layoff that forces us to give pause and take action.

On the other hand, reaching that point can also be more of a gradual process – a season of discontent that eventually wears on us to the point of action. We are no longer willing to stall, or to make promises to not miss any more of those events, or make commitments to have a more normal schedule next year, after this quarter, or after this

71

case – all which diminish our credibility and influence with those around us.

No matter how we reach this point, there is almost always a transition period. There is so much to learn and understand about all that led us to the place we're at. This is often new territory and can feel unsettling at times or even that we are lost in the wilderness. What is the source of my burnout or disengagement? When and how did I begin to lose touch with those around me? When did I lose track of the direction of my life?

In addition to taking inventory, this transitional period requires intentional time and focus to contemplate all the things that we feel are missing from our lives, as well as all the things we want for our future. In this process, we need to understand the

> **Depending on circumstances, the point of transition may be acutely or chronically driven.**

momentum of our lives and what may be trapping us, and we need to be willing to ask and answer some of the "big questions" of life. Only when we have gained sufficient clarity, can we consider our next steps. We can decide to stay on our current path but with some informed adjustments to get us where we want to be. We could also choose to re-target the direction of our lives, or we could choose anything in between.

Making a course correction is not for the faint of heart or those who lack conviction. It can be scary. It takes knowledge and courage. As we work through this process, we need to acknowledge, face, and work past our fears – our contradictory fears of things staying the same and our fears of missing out on a full life. The tug of war between FOTS and FOMO.

Pieces of a Full Life

When we reach or feel ourselves reaching "the point," we know we have some pieces in place, but we also know something is missing or is out of balance that is keeping us from the full life we covet. Our desire for change is most often seeded with early regrets and a fear of having even greater regrets in the future if we stay on this current path. In order to have a full life, we need to identify what is missing and figure out how to connect to it. If our time, energy, and focus are out of balance, we need to figure out ways to rebalance.

A full life can be different for each of us and can change from season to season. It could be spending more time with a spouse and family, connecting more with friends, traveling, having opportunities to personally learn and grow, or having time to invest in our physical and spiritual wellness.

One aspect that can't be denied is that deep and meaningful relationships matter in terms of having a full life... as well as being happier and healthier! In fact, this was also a conclusion of a 75-year study conducted by Harvard University. The study further concluded that the presence of someone we can rely on, trust, and be vulnerable with reduces our emotional as well as physical pain, and that the absence of these types of relationships can lead to earlier declines in our mental and physical health and earlier death. In addition, the people who were most satisfied in their relationships at midlife were the healthiest at age 80. (Harvard Study of Adult Development, 2017; reference 5). The types of relationships matter as well.

Perspectives from Experience

I learned about the power of relationships as I was studying poverty and researching the best ways to help eradicate it as part of our service work. We grew to love the children and the people we were serving. We saw firsthand that we had so much in common. The only major differences were that the people we served had much less than most of us materially and had fewer opportunities. At the same time, however, there were major differences coming in the other direction. Those we served seemed to have a greater sense of community, connectedness, and contentment than many of us serving did. It was clear that they had "less" but also clear they had more overall happiness and joy. That was a paradox for me. It ran counter to my world view at the time and left me perplexed.

Regardless of your definition of a full life, relationships matter.

Being perplexed drove me to better understand poverty. To do so, I again took to available books and books-on-tape. My free time, car time, and walk-around the Eastern Promenade at lunch time were filled with learning. In our service work, we also continually tested and tried what we learned as we enhanced and expanded our offerings. Books like When Helping Hurts *by Steve Corbett and Brian Fikkert and* Toxic Charity *by Robert D. Lupton were a couple of the books that articulated well how a lack of several key relationships all contributed to poverty, and that establishing and strengthening all these relationships is essential to helping to address poverty. It was only partially about money and things. Those would only help address aspects of material poverty. Of equal or even greater importance was a positive sense of self, connections with others, and faith in something greater than ourselves.*

These references validated what we experienced and helped fill in the gaps. The four key relationships essential to addressing poverty included: a relationship with God as a higher power; a positive relationship with ourselves and a sense of purpose; a relationship with others and a sense of belonging within our communities; and a relationship with the world in a way that allows us to be productive and to be able to provide for ourselves and our families. Establishing and strengthening each of these relationships would be the key to addressing all forms of poverty – material, emotional, and spiritual.

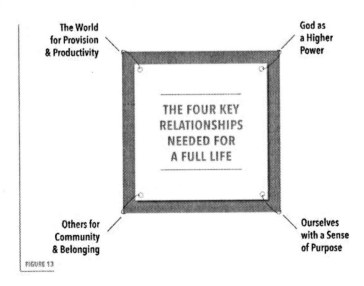

FIGURE 13

These four relationships work in the inverse, too. We experienced this over the years of leading service teams. While many of us were not materially poor, many of us did feel emotional and spiritual deficits. Through our experience and the work of others, the lack of one or more of these key relationships is what leads to discontentment. Establishing and strengthening these four relationships in our lives also leads us to a life with greater joy and contentment.

For many of us, given our committed focus on our crafts and our careers (i.e., our relationship with this world for provision and productivity), we may need to focus more on balancing our investments in the three other relationships in order to win at life in the way we are winning or have won in our careers.

The Comfort, Money, and Momentum Traps

The success we enjoy today is most often a result of our past commitments and investments. As we approach and enter new work and life seasons, there are a number of elements that can hamper our transition and also add to the frustrations that can fuel the burnout-disengagement cycle. Elements such as our comfort, money, and momentum can work against our ability to learn and grow, take on appropriate new risk, and re-target our actions toward the future we desire.

The Comfort Trap:

From a place of comfort, we can often find and tap confidence, strength, and courage. From a place of *too much* comfort or from a place of being comfortable for too long, we can become defensive and inappropriately risk averse – and that can work against or trap us.

Getting comfortable at work is an important element to advancing our careers. From a place of comfort, we can learn, grow, and begin master our craft. Once comfortable with less complicated projects, accounts, cases, surgeries, or curriculum we can move to more complicated ones. As we venture into the unfamiliar environments necessary to pursue the more complicated assignments, we are comforted by the fact we have been successful in the past.

However, too much comfort at work can stall our advancement and even bore us. Once we have achieved a certain level of success, comfort may limit our future growth. In nature, the process of dying begins once growth stops. The same is true for our careers. A lack of growth at work can cause atrophy, make us defensive, and make us inappropriately risk averse, trapping us in our past.

Many of us have been so busy and running at a burnout pace for so long that is has become familiar to us. Even though we don't necessarily like where we're at or the

> *Too much comfort and familiarity can limit growth and make us too risk averse.*

direction our lives have taken, we generally grow comfortable with what is familiar. This is an ironic sense of comfort that can also make us defensive and inappropriately risk averse in terms of initiating change. This can be especially true if we are feeling overwhelmed and isolated due to the burnout-disengagement cycle and losing touch, track, and clarity in our lives.

The Money Trap:

Money can be, and mean, a lot of different things to a lot of different people. Money can be an opportunity, a reward, an expectation, a validation, an identity, or security. Money can be something owned or be something stewarded. Money can unite or money can divide.

Although our reasons may differ, many of us feel financial pressures. It is these pressures that can trap us as we look to successfully transition from one season to the next.

Although we can feel trapped in the short term by our need to pay off college, MBA, law school, medical school, or business loans, or our need to buy a home, raise a family, and begin to save some money, all this is really just part of life – it's what we need to do to take care of ourselves and our families. A benefit most professionals enjoy is a decent salary that can often allow us to accomplish all these things as part of an overall comfortable financial life. Feeling trapped in the short term may temporarily bind us to a particular organization or a career until a loan is paid or we reach another milestone. At that point, we can feel more freedom to choose a pivot.

The money trap seems to be a larger snare during the mid-point and later seasons of our lives. And the biggest culprit is often our lifestyle. Many of us have been fortunate to have improved our lifestyle beyond our basic needs as we work through our "mastering our craft" and "making a name" seasons. This is often very positive and a reward for our commitment and hard work.

As we look at making changes that can allow us to achieve new goals or lead a more fulfilling life, we need to realize that our lifestyles are often addictive. Once established, we will need to be discerning about what we need, what we want, and what traps us, and we need to be diligent about spotting lifestyle creep. We also need to keep in perspective the near constant voices (in media, magazines, and through different advisors)

> *Money can trap us in all seasons without vison and a plan.*

that seemingly only suggest that we work more, save more, and invest more. Yes, we may want to prepare for the ever increasing costs of college to help our children... but our grandchildren? Yes, we may need to prepare for longer and more expensive retirements due to increased life expectancies and health care costs... but also save to leave an inheritance? As it relates to escaping or side-stepping the money trap, we may be best served to attach a specific number and date to the goals so as not to allow our focus to drift only toward ever-larger needs in an ever-distant future such that they trap us *today*.

The power of the money trap is validated by statistics showing that most of us (the 67 percent of us who are disengaged at work) are now staying in jobs we don't enjoy, that are uninspiring, or that fail to offer growth. Our need for money is real, but we shouldn't pack it in and give up pursuing our dreams, achieving our potential, or living a full life just because of the ensnaring nature of money.

Beyond our salaries, organizations can also trap us with money, but this can backfire if burnout and disengagement exist. Organizations conventionally use stock, partnerships, and incentive compensation to help ensure performance and to help bind top talent to the organization. This has historically been a huge win for organizations; however, winning today is far from guaranteed. Solely retaining employees, even top talent, does not ensure engagement and the ability to produce results over the long term. The golden handcuffs are still handcuffs. Organizations utilizing this approach need to be especially concerned with burnout or disengagement. If senior managers and leaders are burned-out and disengaged but are trapped and staying only for the money, how does that inspire and motivate others in your organization? If organizations are not willing to address burnout and disengagement head-on and effectively, conventional retention strategies can hurt organizations from the inside out, and it may not be noticeable for a long time... or until it's too late.

Momentum:

Momentum is the flow of our past and present life as a result of our upbringing, education, career choice, season of life, skills, talents, networks, and experiences – the good and the not-so-good. It has the power of our habits and our history. Unless controlled, momentum takes us forward on the trajectory of our past.

Once a certain level of comfort and success is attained, our momentum is strong and hard to change. When we think about other options to our present situation, it may be hard to imagine making that investment again, especially if we are feeling burned-out and exhausted. Even if we are bored, momentum can keep us planted. We often feel an obligation to the past and feel obligated to maintain aspects of our present for our spouse, family, partners, and peers despite our discontentment and lack of interest or passion.

Altering our momentum can also be further complicated when our work or our organization has become our identity. It can be a long process to unwind this, and it takes a different approach than the one we took to achieve our success. Changing our

> **Understanding and changing our momentum requires increased levels of awareness.**

momentum can require a major personal rebranding effort. But what do we rebrand to? What do we want out of life? What do we want to attain in terms of personal significance?

Perspectives from Experience

Based on my experience, research, and the good counsel of others, I developed a formula that helped me chart a path toward a fuller and more significant life. The formula included gaining a new perspective and redeploying the elements of time, momentum, motivation, and fear.

From the time I knew I wanted to be doing something different from the path I was on, the value I placed on time escalated. As I got older and I watched my kids grow up, it was also more apparent to me that time was not infinite and more of it would never be guaranteed. I had a new sense of urgency about time. However, despite my desire to move ahead and this new perspective on time,

I knew it would be essential for me to slow down first. I wanted my future to be better than my past, and I needed to plan well.

When I advised my partners that I wanted to do something different in five to 10 years, that was a big step. In reality, I needed to take many more big steps to be able to do so. This was likely the reason I felt people didn't believe that I would really leave. A lot was stacked against me. I had comfort professionally in that I was pretty good at my craft and was in a position to control much of what I did at work; it afforded a comfortable lifestyle, and having both those comforts in place helped grow my parallel life. Through the transition process, I came to terms with what I thought of money and its role in influencing my behavior, and I was eventually freed from the money trap. Along the way, I developed several proformas to help me plan a viable exit. Through the process of developing my S-curves, I also became comfortable with my past and my momentum.

Armed with these new perspectives, I was excited to enter a new season and leverage as much of my past as possible in a new context. But I wasn't ready yet. I needed to think through what I really wanted to do, and how I would unwind my present position at work. This all took time.

Establishing and maintaining enough quiet time and space (i.e., margin) was a critical element and it required the most discipline. In order for me to make good progress on my transition plan, I needed to spend at least an hour a day most days of the week, and have at least one day during which I could spend multiple hours reading, mapping, contemplating, and documenting the steps that would be needed.

Spending sufficient time in margin also helped me understand and clarify my motivations. Why did I put so much effort into the first half of my career? Why did I develop such a passion for my parallel life? Did I have something to prove? What parts of my motivations were rooted in money, power, position, and receiving praise, and what parts were an honest desire to serve others? I grew to accept that there were many years of the former but also felt encouraged by a solid move toward the latter. I felt confident that the honest desire to serve was why I was becoming a better leader. Taking into account motivation as part of my self-learning was a mindset shift. Once I better understood motivation, I would spend as much time thinking about why something was happening versus focusing only on what was happening.

I also ended up adjusting my mindset on fear. Previous to my transition, fear was a negative. Fear was something that needed to be suppressed or managed so it didn't hamper or stop my plans. As I worked through my transition, I grew to fear more the status quo and maintaining the momentum of my past than I did stepping out more into the unknown. I began to fear missing out on a full life and my ability to have an impact than I did on further improving my

> **Fear of the status quo is often more damaging than fear of the unknown.**

comfort. I began to fear a future with regrets. As I approached what I saw as a fork in the road, needing to make the final decision on staying in my career or pivoting away, fear was no longer holding me back or trapping me; it was now positive motivation for change.

Looking Forward to the Fork in the Road

Once I began to take ownership of my time, good things started to happen. Following through to process, contemplate, and document where I'd been, where I stood, and where my momentum was taking me was a huge step. The improved self-awareness and the clarity gained through the process gave me comfort. This comfort, combined with a number of mindset shifts, helped launch a series of visions of what the future could hold. Approaching the fork in the road now became exciting.

In all, it took seven years from my time of sensing discontent for the first time in 2009 to my exit becoming reality in 2016. At least two of those years were focused on trying to make things work at the office, and five years were spent trying to figure out exactly what I would be doing in the future – outside of the office. The last two years were the most intense.

The mindset shift over fear was as important as improving my self-awareness and gaining clarity. With fear as additional currency, I felt as though I had the keys to all the traps and the keys to open new doors as I explored my future options.

Exploring my options ranged from taking on higher positions at work to be able to more easily influence change to redesigning my current role to accomplish more of the things aligned with my interests. Once I became convinced that the platform at the office wouldn't work, my options expanded to the nonprofit space with which I had become familiar. I loved the work we were doing in our organization and saw much more potential. For several years, we successfully worked to grow and expand the organization and its offerings. I even went back to school to earn an Executive Certificate in Transformational Nonprofit Leadership. As rewarding as this was (and continues to be), I continued to think there was more.

Although, I wasn't inspired in my job as it was, I did still like certain aspects of it. I loved the creative and strategic aspects of solving problems and designing solutions. I enjoyed the challenge of solving existing problems, and I relished opportunities to create new approaches with a blank sheet of paper. Through all my personal growth and exploration, I had come to realize that the only thing that changed were the types of problems I was interested in solving. I came to realize I was most interested in solving people problems, and I didn't want to be limited in how to address them. This realization was actually a relief. I had been concerned that the first half of my career was just something I was going to do until I figured out the other thing I wanted to do… but now I saw my engineering career as an integral part of my future.

> *Our history plays an important role in our future.*

In addition to still being inspired by problem solving and solutions design, I'd grown to appreciate the power of business. Business done well creates tremendous value and opportunity. It has the power to solve problems and create positive change. Business done well can inspire creativity and productivity and provide us freedom to pursue a full life. I saw this in my own life, and I saw this in the lives of others at home and in the developing world. The promise of business done well is universal. That realization was one of the last pieces to fall into place for me. I loved the promise of business and what that could do to solve people problems both inside and outside of organizations.

The future is our opportunity to live the life we want. The key aspect is being able to figure out what we want. Burnout and disengagement can capture us, busyness can take from us, and comfort, money, and momentum can trap us... but a full life still calls us and fear can be overcome. We know this is true because most of us feel that things today are not quite right. We know there just has to be a better way, and we hear that "still small voice" inside encouraging us. We need to take ownership of our lives. Our future can take a long time to develop and it needs to begin now. There is too much on the line right now for many of us to wait until after the next assignment or after the next quarter. Time is ticking and tomorrow is not guaranteed.

As individuals, we need to own our time now as a first step and begin to figure out what we want. We need to work to make sure we maximize the return on all our past investments – at work and in life.

As organizations, we need to realize that all employees, but especially top talent, see a fork in the road coming. Whether it be the result of burnout and disengagement, transition to a new season, or just a desire for more growth and opportunity, the fork is a transition point when action will be taken to decide what the future will hold. It can be a decision to pivot away, or it can be a decision to try to adjust our present circumstances and refresh in place.

> *When we reach the fork, we need to decide whether to stay the course, refresh in place, or pivot away.*

Top organizations and leaders realize the importance of understanding both the realities of work and life today, as well as what top employees are looking for, and then offering them choices to allow them to immediately engage and grow in place in ways that are aligned with the organization's interests and goals and create at least a win-win.

Key Points

- Whether we come up on it quickly or see it gradually appear on the horizon, we eventually reach a point where we need to take action – a fork in the road where we need to make a decision about the path of our future.
- As we approach the point of action, we can feel trapped between contradictory fears – fear of the same – FOTS – or fear of missing out – FOMO.
- No matter how we define a full life, relationships matter. Four key relationships that fill deficits and create abundance

include a relationship with God as a higher power, a positive relationship with ourselves with a sense of purpose, a relationship with others for community and belonging, and a relationship with the world for provision and productivity.

- Comfort, money, and momentum can also form traps that we need to understand in order to release us from their hold or side-step their attempt to ensnare us.

- The road leading up to the fork can be exciting if we take the time to understand where we've been, where we stand, where our momentum is taking us, and gain greater clarity and self-awareness. These steps will also make our decisions easier.

- Top organizations and leaders realize the importance of understanding both the realities of work and life today, as well as what top employees are looking for, and then offering them choices to allow them to immediately engage and grow in place in ways that are aligned with the organization's interests and goals and create at least a win-win.

Part 2:

What Top Employees Want

Top employees today want to have it all.

Having it all includes having financial success. Total financial freedom would be great but may not be realistic for most of us. But partial financial freedom – the kind that affords us some flexibility beyond our basic needs and our nice-to-haves – is both desirable and achievable.

Whether we figured it out the hard way or were able to discover it through others, many of us today are shooting higher than mere financial success and its shortcomings and trappings. Financial success, however, can be a key milestone en route to a greater destination.

In addition to some financial freedom, top employees want greater meaning in their lives and purpose in their work. Top employees also do not want to stop growing once they have mastered their craft and made a name for themselves. These accomplishments are also just milestones. Top employees want to build on those milestones in order to become the full person they were meant to be... and have the impact in life they were meant to have.

These wants are not simply the dreams of our past, captured in our senior quote or college essay and then forgotten. Our dreams are wired within us. Sure, the grind of 8:00 a.m. classes and finals weeks, figuring out what we're going to do after college, and then landing that first job may have buried them a little. And yes, the 10, 20, or even 30 years of mastering our craft, making a name, and raising a family, may have buried them a bit deeper, but they are still there. They are there when we take the time to reflect, and they are often there at the root of our frustrations related to work and life. This is why many of us find ourselves at or approaching a point of seemingly dramatic action.

So other than financial success and greater meaning, purpose, and growth, what do top employees want? First, they want a little help managing the realities of work and life today. We, including top employees, want more flexibility and control over our time so that we can better integrate and balance all that we want to accomplish. We also want some help keeping our perspectives. We could use some wise counsel and coaching on how to best prioritize and transition between seasons. In our world of busyness, we want to be reminded from time to time of the big picture and the goals that matter most, not just what it's going to take to meet this quarter's budget. We want to maximize our ability to achieve our goals today but not at the expense of our dreams or our future. Top employees will not settle forever. If we don't get help from the organization, we are certainly capable of getting it ourselves. It may take a while to get out of the burnout-disengagement cycle, but top employees eventually will.

In the previous section, I shared what can happen when leaders and organizations fail to address burnout and disengagement, but what if "a little help" along with the opportunities for reward and greater meaning, purpose, and growth are provided rather than forcing or waiting for top employees to figure it out themselves? Well, there is a tremendous upside for those willing and courageous enough to provide it.

There is still more, however. Top employees today are interested in developing their own brand and their own platform. They want to have an identity and stand for something – their brand. They want to have a setting or a stage where they can share what they have to offer and deliver the impact they want to have at work... and in life – their platform. This is a mindset top leaders and organizations need to embrace when dealing with top talent. Top leaders and organizations will learn to leverage this rather than fall prey to our natural tendency to be threatened by it. Top leaders and organizations will leverage it by designing opportunities to align brands and platforms and to co-create opportunities, products, and services that work for all – including clients, customers, patients, etc.

Knowing what top employees want, top leaders and organizations will treat top employees as cherished volunteers and donors. They will also embrace the security top employees feel when their careers are portable. As a result, they will work to inspire engagement and build trust. The power has shifted.

Today, it is the role of leaders and organizations to inspire engagement and build trust. It is an employee's decision whether what's offered is motivation enough to be retained... or whether the trust extended is authentic enough to build loyalty, respect, and even reverence. Whether or not an employee stays or decides to pivot away, it will always be in the leaders' and organizations' best interest to embrace both the decision and the person.

This is what top employees want. Sound familiar?

Chapter Four:

Success +

The definition of success today is being redefined and expanded. Top talent is looking for the financial success we have traditionally associated with "success"... plus more.

The new definition of success is more fluid and adjusts between work and life seasons. The new definition of success has expanded beyond serving the organization and even beyond advancing our career interests. The new definition of success includes having a career with meaning and purpose and winning at both work and life. We want to be able to excel on all fronts – and in all seasons. And at the end of our efforts, or as we transition from one season to the next, we want to feel content. We want to know we did our best and made an impact.

In terms of success, winning and contentment are outcomes – we can't just step into them. In a business context, enjoying profits and a thriving culture are also outcomes that we desire, and similarly, we can't just step into those either.

Achieving these outcomes follows a logic model: Outcomes result from a specific set of inputs aligned with well-designed activities that then produce a series of targeted outputs that amass to realize desired outcomes. Successful outcomes often require intentional planning and effective execution.

In a work context, employees are specific "inputs." Given the nature of people, there can be much complexity in the workplace, but there are many common and unifying elements that contribute to successful outcomes that resonate with all employees, especially those with top talent.

Traditional Success

Let's first get the financial aspects of success off the table. Employee compensation needs to be aligned with the value provided to an organization, and in almost every case, this will be a non-negotiable. An employee's need for appropriate financial reward is a basic motivation behind our work and our careers in order to have the resources to take care of ourselves and our families, as well as to provide a platform to help us achieve bigger dreams. Organizations that pay fairly for the value delivered have much to gain in terms of being able to grow and profit through employee performance to deliver value to the organization.

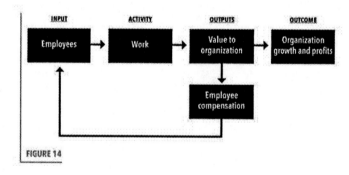

Figure 14 illustrates the basic logic model for work.

In this basic model, compensation is an output directed toward employees as a catalyst for work necessary to deliver value to clients, customers, and patients in order to grow and profit the organization.

So, should employees been seen as a cost or an asset? How leaders and organizations answer this question has a major role in determining their own outcome and success over the long term. A cost-based approach could help win a quarterly battle or two or help with a year-over-year comparison, but that approach will not produce a victory in the "talent war." Winning this war needs to be the focus of all organizations that want to succeed, especially those in professional services – that only have *talent* to sell. An investment mindset and actual investment actions are necessary in order to even compete in the talent war today.

> *Competing in the talent war requires both an investment mindset and action.*

Top leaders and organizations will ensure compensation is at least fair in order to take the money question "off the table." They understand that it will be counterproductive to have top talent reminded every two weeks or at the end of every year of any pay inequity. Instead, their goal should be to "free" talent to be able to focus on their revenue-producing activities. In addition, organizations with an inequitable approach to compensation set off red flags for top talent prompting them to ask: "Are leaders out of touch? Does the organization have a scarcity mindset? Is the business model flawed? Is there really an opportunity for growth here?"

However, even fair compensation may not be enough to inspire higher levels of performance with 67 percent disengagement in the workplace today. Something else is clearly needed. This was certainly the case with me, and according to the 2017 Gallup State of the American Workplace report, this is the case for most of us. Today, most of us are also looking for our work to have meaning and purpose.

Meaning and Purpose

Meaning and purpose in the workplace is powerful. Meaning and purpose is powerful and tangible primarily because it fuels employee engagement.

Employee engagement is the subject of much buzz and attention today – and for good reason. Unfortunately, most often leaders and organizations take the wrong approach to employee engagement. Most organizations treat engagement as a "thing." Ironically, it is a "thing" for organizations, but it is not a thing for employees – it is both a mindset and a state of being. As a result, there is a fundamental disconnect between engagement in the eyes of organizations and those of employees.

Employee engagement is not about the organization or its leaders. Employee engagement is not even simply about the work and the work environment. Employee engagement also pertains to how the work and the work environment supports, encourages, and enables the interests and passions of an employee. For organizations to have employee engagement, they need to create "engagement for employees." Employee engagement is about investing. The good news is that there is a high return on investment for organizations when "it" is done well.

Engagement for Organizations: Employee engagement is essential for organizational success, especially those employing professionals. Employee engagement is most often the catalyst for improvements in quality and performance that lead the way to greater growth and profits. These improvements increase the value delivered through successful projects and cases, treated patients, educated students, and sold products. It is also employee engagement that helps create cultures that can attract, retain, grow, and further engage.

TARGET LOGIC MODEL FOR WORK TODAY

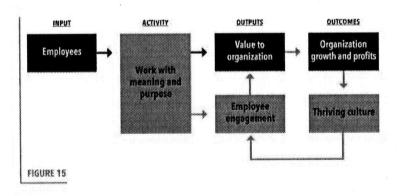

Figure 15 illustrates an ideal logic model for work today.

In the target model, employees are fundamentally considered assets, and the work and the work environment (i.e., the work activities) are designed to engage and invest in those assets. The result is a new flow within an organization that works to reinforce positive outputs and outcomes. Employee engagement is the key output to achieving this positive and reinforcing flow.

The key to employee engagement, however, is work with meaning and purpose. An organization can contribute to this with an attractive mission, vision, and values statement, but it also needs to deliver. If the realities of the office don't resemble the promises, or, if for one reason or another, these are not lived by or lived by consistently, there won't be a desirable work environment and there won't be employee engagement. "If you're going to talk the talk, you've got to walk the walk."

For most organizations to achieve the type of engagement that can create the positive and reinforcing flow, they will need to have several elements in place: First, they will need a strong and attractive mission, vision, and values statement; second, they will need to live by it, even if that means redesigning the workplace;

> *Employee engagement requires attractive mission, vision, and values; a desirable work environment; and a deep understanding of employees.*

and third, they will need to go deeper to better understand their employees.

Engagement for Employees: For employees, engagement at work is both a state of mind and being that is influenced by the realities we face in work and life.

All things being equal, working for a reputable organization with a strong and attractive mission, vision, and values statement in a field we have pursued would yield employee engagement.

EMPLOYEE ENGAGEMENT- ALL THINGS BEING EQUAL

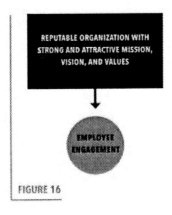

Figure 16 illustrates employee engagement for this scenario.

The reality, however, is all things are not always equal. So where do we go from here in terms of understanding employee engagement?

Perspectives from Experience

That was the question I asked myself too late in the burnout and disengagement process. I asked that question long after I had made the decision to pivot. Despite the fact that I know it was the right decision for me, and I am very happy I made it, I always knew it didn't need to be that way. There were ways to make it all work. I knew there would be a way to reverse engineer a process that would immediately re-engage me back into my organization and my career.

The re-engineering of the new way began with understanding all the elements and the gaps that contributed to my precipitous loss of engagement after many years at extremely high levels down to the point at which I decided to pivot away. My goal with this book and related coaching, consulting, training, and speaking is to help other talented professionals, leaders, and business owners better understand and grow employee engagement as a component of the process to reverse burnout in ways that benefit both the individual and the organization.

Designing Engagement

Interests: Our professional and personal interests play a major role in determining engagement. Although interests certainly vary from person to person, top talent is typically unified by: doing excellent work; working with others who are committed to excellent work; the opportunity to do what they do best every day; opportunities to grow and advance; working with people they like in a friendly, supportive, engaging, and even fun atmosphere; and having a life and having an impact beyond the office walls. All employees, and especially top talent, are also unified in what they are ***not*** interested in, and this includes: prolonged work overload, unaddressed workplace frustrations, personal frustrations from work/life imbalance, and burnout.

SUMMARY OF GENERAL UNIFYING
INTERESTS DETERMINATE TO ENGAGEMENT

WHAT TOP TALENT IS INTERESTED IN:

○ Doing excellent work

○ Working with others committed to excellent work

○ Opportunity to do what they do best every day

○ Opportunities to grow and advance

○ Work with people they like in a friendly, supportive,
   engaging, and even fun atmosphere

○ Have a life beyond work

○ Have an impact beyond work

WHAT TOP TALENT IS NOT INTERESTED IN:

○ Prolonged work overload

○ Unaddressed workplace frustrations

○ Personal frustrations from missing out

○ Burnout

FIGURE 17

A summary of these general unifying interests is presented as Figure 17.

Specific interests are also a determinant. Our specific interests vary between our work and life seasons and as we transition between them.

SUMMARY OF TYPICAL SPECIFIC
INTERESTS DETERMINANT TO ENGAGEMENT

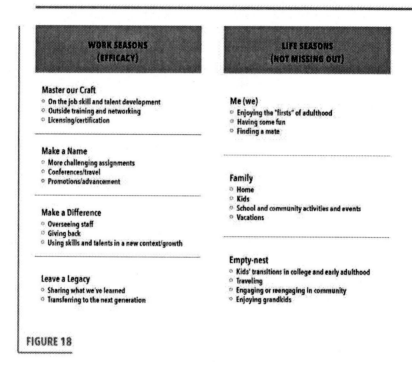

**WORK SEASONS
(EFFICACY)**

Master our Craft
- On the job skill and talent development
- Outside training and networking
- Licensing/certification

Make a Name
- More challenging assignments
- Conferences/travel
- Promotions/advancement

Make a Difference
- Overseeing staff
- Giving back
- Using skills and talents in a new context/growth

Leave a Legacy
- Sharing what we've learned
- Transferring to the next generation

**LIFE SEASONS
(NOT MISSING OUT)**

Me (we)
- Enjoying the "firsts" of adulthood
- Having some fun
- Finding a mate

Family
- Home
- Kids
- School and community activities and events
- Vacations

Empty-nest
- Kids' transitions in college and early adulthood
- Traveling
- Engaging or reengaging in community
- Enjoying grandkids

FIGURE 18

Examples of some of the more typical interests specific to each season are summarized in Figure 18.

Passions: In addition to our interests, our passions play a role in our level of engagement at work. Our passions attach meaning to our interests, and the meaning we attach dictates the priority and the energy we place on and commit to that interest.

THE ROLE OF PASSION IN DETERMINING THE PRIORITY AND ENERGY GIVEN TO INTERESTS

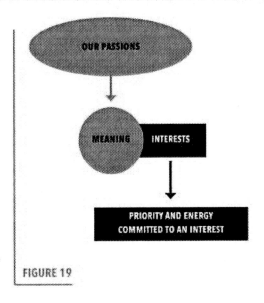

FIGURE 19

This role passion plays in determining the priority and energy given an interest is illustrated in Figure 19.

Many of us had a passion for mastering our craft and making a name early in our careers. To this end, we attached meaning to our career development and advancement. Our passion enabled us to work all those crazy hours to impress the boss and secure that next opportunity and then repeat the cycle until we achieved the goals associated with that interest.

As we progress in life, interests grow. As we are making our name at the office, we may also be raising a family at home. Even today, some organizations dictate at least an informal or subtle choice of one over the other. Many of us may have had to drop our kids off at daycare and routinely work nights and weekends in order to pursue our work interests. Others may have chosen to take some time off, work part-time, or job-share for a season to pursue our family interests. Having to choose one or the other limits the prospects for engagement. Today, most top talent has an interest – and a passion – to try to excel at both home and the office. Organizations that are willing and able to support, encourage, and enable this will open up channels for engagement.

> *Top talent wants to excel inside and outside the office, and organizations who deliver will earn engagement.*

As we mature in life and grow in self- and social-awareness, our interests and the passion behind them change and evolve. Our ability to see and understand these changes will be a determinant in both our engagement at the office and our contentedness in life. The greater our self-awareness, the more proactive and effective we can be in achieving the life we desire and design.

An organization's self- and "employee-awareness" will determine its ability to adapt to both accommodate the changes in interests and passions to encourage engagement as well as the organization's ability to leverage and grow through these changes. Top organizations will also anticipate employee changes and offer adaptive win-win models that will encourage engagement as well as boost loyalty and goodwill.

The presence of burnout and disengagement, of course, changes everything. Before the benefit of any of the above can be realized, burnout needs to be reversed. Once reversed, we can then begin to rediscover our passions.

Discovering or rediscovering our passions is a process that takes time. It takes time because our passions are ultimately tied to purpose. That said, the identification of purpose being the ultimate driver of our passions may not be immediately helpful. The word purpose seems to have so many meanings that it has lost significance. The actual definition of purpose doesn't help either in terms of providing an easy answer. *Merriam-Webster* defines purpose as: "something set up as an object or end to be attained." That seems definitive, but in terms of applying it to our lives, the definition itself lends to confusion as "something" can be anything and because there is no time dimension.

Perspectives from Experience

As I worked through the process to understand what drove my passions through different seasons, I found that I had understood and used "purpose" in three different ways. The first was "having something serve a purpose," the second was "finding a purpose in something," and the third was in "discovering my purpose."

The first two examples utilized something as a means to an end, and not the object or end itself. As an example going wwaaayy back: Beginning in sixth grade, I wanted spending money. Whether it was to go to the movies or roller skating or buy some new cassettes, I needed some cash. As a means to that cash, I chose to wake up before dawn most mornings and deliver newspapers. My paper route served a purpose. However, I also found personal value in my paper route. Getting up early every morning or trudging through rain and snow before school wasn't always enjoyable, but I did appreciate the new relationships, skills, self-esteem, and independence it was able to deliver – so I also found purpose in my paper route. In contrast, "discovering my purpose" over the past decade was the object or end I wanted to attain.

APPLYING PURPOSE TO OUR LIVES

FORMS OF PURPOSE	MEANS TO AN OBJECT OR END	OBJECT OR END ITSELF
Having something serve a purpose	✓	
Finding a purpose in something	✓	
Discovering our life purpose		✓

FIGURE 20

A summary of these forms of purpose is presented in Figure 20.

The confusion around "career and purpose" begins to set in around the time we succeed in mastering our craft and making our name. These were the "somethings" or the objects we set out to attain. But after we check that box, then what? Even without the layers of busyness, burnout, and disengagement that afflict many of us, we may very well grow bored with our careers after reaching this level of success.

The source of confusion is that we have elevated and misplaced expectations about what a career can deliver. Even with continual growth, our career is unlikely to also double as the purpose for our lives. For most of us, that will be a false promise. Certainly, our career could be an important aspect, and it could provide major leverage points, paths, and opportunities for us, but we have a life outside of the office that matters, too.

The fact is that most of us will need to expand beyond our offices as we know them in order

> *Although important, our career alone is not likely to double as our life purpose.*

to live a full life and discover the purpose for our lives. Our life purpose will be the ultimate driver of our passions, particularly in the second half of our adult lives. In addition, not living in the flow or pursuit of our life purpose will be a source of our discontent.

Knowing this to be true, top organizations will redesign and expand the workplace in order to promote and encourage the development of emotional intelligence and the pursuit of purpose. In addition, top organizations will intentionally seek and align with opportunities to grow with and through the changing and evolving interests and passions of top talent.

REVERSE ENGINEERING ELEMENTS
DETERMINANT TO EMPLOYEE ENGAGEMENT

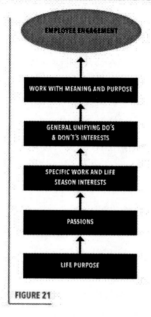

FIGURE 21

A summary of all of the elements determinant to employee engagement is illustrated in Figure 21.

Organizations need to understand that an employee's engagement can be derailed if any of these elements aren't in place. The good news, however, is that informed and proactive organizations can play a major role in keeping the opportunities for engagement on track and attractive. Additionally, these opportunities enhance employees' levels of contentment.

Contentment

Being contented, which *Merriam-Webster* defines as: "feeling or showing satisfaction with one's possessions, status, or situation," is an outcome. Again, we can't simply step into it. Contentment is similar to employee engagement in terms of being a state of mind and being – but on the much broader scale of life.

The type of success top talent seeks today is one that leads to contentment, not continual striving or mere happiness in the moment. Once attained, contentment can be enjoyed every day – even as we battle through the ups and downs of our pursuit of purpose and winning at work and life.

Key Points

- Along with fair compensation, top talent wants work to have meaning and purpose.
- Meaning and purpose at work is powerful and tangible because it fuels employee engagement.
- Employee engagement is not about organizations or their leaders, it is not even about the work or the work environment; it pertains to how the work and the work environment support, encourage, and enable the interests and passions of employees.
- Employee engagement requires attractive mission, vision, and values; a desirable environment; and a deep understanding of employees.
- Today, top talent has an interest and passion for winning at both work and life. Organizations that support, encourage, and enable this open up channels for engagement.

- Self-awareness is the key to understanding interests and the passions behind them.
- An organization's self- and employee-awareness determines its ability to successfully adapt to changes in employee interests and passions.
- Our life purpose is the ultimate driver of our passions, particularly in the second half of our adult lives.
- Top organizations will redesign and expand the workplace to encourage the development of emotional intelligence and the pursuit of purpose. They will also intentionally seek opportunities to align growth with the interests and passions of top talent.
- The type of success top talent seeks today is one that leads to contentment that we can enjoy every day.

Chapter Five:

A Little Help

We live in a 24-hour world today, and because of technology, work insidiously creeps into it well outside of the time we spend in the office. The traditional 8-to-5 or 9-to-5 is over, and the reality we face today as a result is rampant (and growing!) burnout and disengagement.

Now, leaders and organizations have a choice to make: Stay with the status quo or create a new reality that supports, encourages, and enables growth and success. Creating a new reality requires intentional planning and investment but begins by providing top talent with a little help as they venture through the new landscape created by increased technology and connectivity.

Flexibility

A typical workday for many professionals and business owners yields little to no personal time before, during, and after work. On top of this, we often go into the weekend with a deficit and end them early to prepare for the upcoming week. "Living to work" is not the life top talent desires. Flexibility in terms of both time and choice is needed to achieve success today.

Flexibility is needed to have better work-life balance to allow us to meet all of our basic life needs and obligations. Flexibility is also needed to create the conditions that allow top talent to excel as well as successfully transition between seasons.

Work-Life Balance: The demands of work and life vary and can ebb and flow with and against each other. Top talent needs work scheduling flexibility to meet life needs and obligations. Trying to meet personal needs and obligations without schedule flexibility adds stress to the workweek and reduces prospects of being able to rest and recharge on the weekends – essential for long-term well-being and productivity.

Some common life needs and obligations that work flexibility can help address include:

- Personal appointments and errands: Many must be scheduled Monday through Friday.
- Child care: Can involve specific day-of-the-week needs, pick-up and drop-off coordination, responding to sick days, snow days, half days, teacher days, field trips, and school vacations.
- Elder and other family care: Can involve coordination and attendance for visitations, appointments, and errands.
- Personal activities and events: After-school and early evening community-based events, time for family and friends, routine date nights with spouse, and planning and coordination related to birthdays, anniversaries, and holidays.

Several generally accepted flexible work strategies to address basic life needs and obligations include:

- Work-from-home: Can add time to our days that would otherwise be consumed by commuting and allow us to be physically present to facilitate needed care.

- Flexible in-office work schedule: Can optimize commutes and personal creative periods.
- Shortened workweeks: Can be accommodated with the use of nine nine-hour workdays followed by a weekday off every other week or with the use of four 10-hour days with a weekday off each week. These options produce at least two to four extra personal days per month for needs and obligations or for longer weekends and additional relaxation and rejuvenation time.

TYPICAL LIFE NEEDS AND OBLIGATIONS, AND FLEXIBLE WORK STRATEGIES TO ADDRESS

BASIC LIFE NEEDS AND OBLIGATIONS	WORK FROM HOME	FLEXIBLE IN-OFFICE TIME	SHORTENED WORKWEEKS
Personal errands and appointments	✓	✓	✓
Child-care	✓	✓	✓
Elder and other family-care	✓	✓	✓
Personal activities and events	✓	✓	✓

FIGURE 22

A summary of typical basic life needs and obligations and flexible work strategies that can be employed is presented in Figure 22.

As shown, each strategy has the potential to meet basic life needs and obligations. However, depending on personal circumstances, one option or a combination of options may best meet the needs and obligations of different employees.

Excelling at Work and Life: Excelling at work and life requires that we create space for rest and rejuvenation at night, on weekends, and during vacations. Sufficient rest and rejuvenation is critical to maintaining consistent performance at the office, and time away from the office is critical to establishing and maintaining meaningful relationships. Yet, we don't always exact the discipline to practice this ourselves or encourage this organizationally in the face of day-to-day and week-to-week goals and priorities. This needs to change if we want top talent to excel. Additionally, organizations may need to actually encourage (and possibly demand) that top talent uses their personal time off if they are failing to honor their own work-life balances.

FLEXIBLE WORK STRATEGIES TO EXCEL
AT WORK AND LIFE TODAY

○ Rest and rejuvenation at night, on weekends, and during vacations

○ De-fragmentation of work days to allow time to concentrate, contemplate, plan, and decompress

○ Periodic retreats

○ Opportunities to experience work in new contexts

○ Sabbaticals

FIGURE 23

A summary of flexible work strategies to excel at work and life today is presented in Figure 23.

Top leaders and organizations will go further to employ processes and systems to help defragment workdays that are becoming more and more cluttered with email and meetings to allow appropriate time to concentrate, contemplate, and plan activities and even decompress after particularly stressful meetings or activities. This is especially important for high-performing professionals and business owners. Top leaders and organizations will also move toward designing periodic retreats, opportunities to experience work in new contexts, and sabbaticals that serve as catalysts for both professional and personal reflection, rejuvenation, and growth.

Successful Transitions to and between New Seasons: During certain seasons or following certain events, work flexibility is wanted or needed. Top leaders and organizations will embrace this and provide choices for top talent during these transitions. The alternative that favors an "either you're here and all in or you're not or not committed" approach puts the organization at risk of employee burnout, disengagement, and loss of talent and institutional knowledge.

For certain seasons and circumstances, top talent may best be served by going part-time. A part-time choice with benefits during these times is an investment that would be most attractive to top talent and would very likely yield return in improved productivity, increased loyalty, and retention. Job-sharing is another form of part-time flexibility that can be attractive, which can have the added benefits of enhancing relationships and culture while also improving organizational resiliency.

Work flexibility is also needed as we transition between seasons. There are significant changes in our interests and passions as we progress through life. Successful transitions into new seasons, particularly those between the first and second halves of adult life (i.e., transitioning from the making a name to the making a difference season and from the family to the empty-nest season), require increases in our emotional intelligence and particularly those aspects related to self-awareness.

> *Successfully transitioning between seasons requires greater awareness and flexibility.*

Work flexibility can aid the process of self-discovery (and rediscovery) that can also lead to greater performance, loyalty, and retention if relationships between top talent and leadership are strong and productive. In such settings, work flexibility can include choices to develop new skills, migration toward and away from certain tasks, and opportunities to participate in new experiences in new environments in order to enhance learning and growth. These could also include participating in periodic retreats, opportunities to experience work in new contexts, and sabbaticals as flexible work strategies that allow us to excel at work and life today as presented earlier.

Better Integration and Boundaries

Work flexibility helps create physical spaces and boundaries to allow better work-life balance. However, that is not enough today since technology and social media comingles and entangles our office and home lives at virtually anytime and anyplace. In order to achieve success, we need to take control and construct virtual spaces and boundaries. To do so, how we access and use technology and social media will need to be reformulated in order to better integrate them in our work and life settings for the benefit and advancement of both the employee and the organization.

> *Success requires the creation and enforcement of boundaries.*

Better integration will result from better understanding goals and priorities. Better integration allows us the time and space to minimize multitasking and the consequences associated with not being fully present in tasks and while spending time with others. The science is increasingly clear that we are much more productive and connect better when we can concentrate and be present – whether at the office or at home.

In order to create and enforce healthy boundaries, we also need to value our time. We need to guard and protect our time as a critical means to accomplish our goals and realize the success we seek. We need to have a sense of urgency in that our time can run out at any time – we have no guarantees for tomorrow. As such, short of emergencies or agreed-to periods to meet specific objectives, boundaries need to be respected and honored, so our time can be deployed in a way that best meets goals.

Coaching

Executive, business, and life coaching is now prevalent and an accepted form of investment to help develop one's capabilities and understandings. Coaching is also regaining ground as a performance management technique inside organizations. Coaching is particularly suited for professionals and business owners because we are capable and proven achievers. Well-designed and effective coaching programs can also be a mechanism for leaders and organizations to build more productive relationships with top talent.

Ambition, commitment, ownership, and excellence are all good – until those begin to hurt us or others. Top talent doesn't want to continually grind toward one aspect of success right up until receiving a "wake-up call" or realizing we have arrived at the fork in the road with no plan and mounting regrets.

Professionals and business owners will flourish through a process that helps them think through their goals, identify the reality of their situation and hurdles they face, layout the options, and develop the steps forward that best meet their unique circumstances. What *won't* bring out their best or keep many around in their second half are monthly, quarterly, or annual meetings that only give directions. What also *won't* work is taking advantage of top talent's drive and ambition, especially during the early years.

Top leaders and organizations will invest in their human capital assets to enable them to grow and produce value by playing the long game to help guide top talent to victories during all seasons. In so doing, top leaders and organizations will help remind employees to keep track of where they stand in pursuit of their work and life goals and coach them through the process of balancing near-term realities with longer-term goals and navigating with or against acceptable norms in order to best achieve those goals.

Effective coaching to create or leverage work flexibility, to better integrate, and establish boundaries will benefit organizations immediately and over the long term. Even if talent eventually pivots, effective coaching can help create long-term brand and organization ambassadors.

Key Points

- The traditional 8-to-5 or 9-to-5 is over and there is no going back – unless we reconstruct a version fit for our lives that we are willing to defend.

- Work flexibility in terms of both time and choice is needed today for work-life balance, to excel at work and life, and as we transition to and between seasons.
- The prevalence of technology and social media requires that we also create virtual spaces and boundaries to support and enhance success.
- Top leaders and organizations today will trust and coach more and direct less.

Chapter Six:

A Winning Brand and Expanding Platform

Today, organizations are placing more emphasis on establishing a winning brand and expanding platform in order to compete and win. This is also the case for top talent.

The brand- and platform-building movements are here to stay. These movements are supported by social shifts, social media, the gig economy, and business at large. For individuals, they have become part of the formula for winning at work and life. Even more importantly, they have also become essential forms of security in a world that is increasingly more volatile and less secure.

The fact that both organizations and individuals participate in the brand and platform movements creates opportunity. The first opportunity centers on alignment. Other opportunities include co-creating and co-branding. Respecting and supporting talent's desire for more control and security is also an opportunity to reverse burnout and improve engagement.

Alignment

There are different groups and forces at play in the work environment. The first step in aligning them is to recognize and understand all of the contributing elements – the different roles and responsibilities at the office as well as the talent's different seasons, interests, and passions. Top leaders and organizations will invest in knowing, discerning and aligning these elements to work well and complement each other.

Brand Alignment: Our brand is our story. It develops over the course of our lives and takes into account the good and the less than good. Our ideal brand is our best and unique self. It is what we want to represent and stand for, and it very likely expands beyond our work identity. Our true brand can only be known and refined through self-awareness and self-mastery.

Brand alignment can begin with an organization's mission, vision, and values statement, but beyond that, top talent wants to be able to win within the organization. Moreover, top talent wants the winning to align with the organization's brand – its measure of authenticity – and also align with their personal brand.

Similar to success, "winning" has now been redefined and expanded. Traditional "bottom line" winning is important; there is no doubt about that – but that is not enough for top talent. For an organization's winning to attract long-term, it needs to evolve and expand beyond tradition. This is especially true for top talent in their second half and those newer to the workplace. Top talent has little interest in winning and profitability that only pads returns for a few at the top and its shareholders.

Top talent sees the world with a stakeholder mindset. Obviously, top leaders and shareholders are stakeholders – but top talent sees more. Top talent sees themselves as key stakeholders – and they are, especially in the world of professional services. Top talent also sees the communities in which we live, work, play, and serve as stakeholders. The type of winning top talent wants to be associated and aligned with is one that invests heavily in its talent as its "greatest asset" as well as one that re-invests in the communities and conditions that enables ongoing success.

> *Today's stakeholders must include more than management and shareholders.*

Top talent wants to be associated with organizations that do more than just consume. They want to be part of organizations that understand, appreciate, and show gratitude toward the conditions that enable the very success they enjoy. Top talent knows success doesn't happen in a vacuum. The opportunity to leverage good ideas and personal drive only exists to the extent there is capital, the rule of law, safe places to work, and talented and motivated people to produce. If we didn't have access to capital to finance our education, car, home, and business, how much success would we have? If we didn't live in a free, open, and generally stable society, how profitable would we be? If we felt unsafe at home or at work, how much could we focus? If we had less opportunity or less influence from others, how much of our talent would we have developed and how motivated would we be to use our talent to excel?

Top talent wants to be able to "pay success forward" and have an impact outside of work... and wants to align with leaders and organizations that want to do the same.

Platform Alignment: Our platform is our stage. It's where we perform and have impact. As our professional and personal lives become more intertwined, our platform needs to follow suit. We typically build our platform during the first half of our lives but begin to recognize and more purposefully operate from it as we get older and transition into later seasons. In this sense, our platform needs to continually expand.

As top talents' desire for impact expands beyond career and immediate family and friends, organizations have a golden opportunity to capitalize on this desire by designing a platform to support, encourage, and enable alignment within the context of the workplace.

Co-Creation and Co-Branding

Where alignment exists, engagement is possible, and when engagement is possible, so is co-creation and co-branding. Co-creation and co-branding take teamwork and collaboration to a new level as it intersects with the new "iWork" and "iLife" trends.

Teamwork and collaboration are major shifts that have taken hold across many types of organizations but even more so in professional services. Cooperative or co-learning has become increasingly important in helping organizations leverage knowledge and create value for those they serve. Co-learning environments also help individuals professionally grow in terms of mastering and refining their craft. Co-learning, however, is most often limited to the workplace – and that is often not enough to fully engage top talent.

Co-Creation: Co-creation typically involves bringing an organization and its clients together with a shared purpose to create better products, outcomes, and experiences. Done well, the co-creation process increases engagement and promises to deliver higher value and more customized solutions to increasingly complex problems. Done well, co-creation also generates greater organization-client buy-in to approaches and ownership of solutions. Professionally speaking, co-creation feeds top talents' appetite to have a unique role and contribution at the office. This is the "iWork" phenomenon.

Co-creation can also work internally in an organization – especially as leaders and talent look to address burnout and disengagement. Top talent has much to offer in terms of creating or redesigning work and a work environment that enables the winning sought today. This customization of personal and professional success is the "iLife" phenomenon.

Organizationally speaking, co-creation with top talent to address burnout and disengagement

> *Co-creation promotes buy-in and ownership and sets the stage for co-branding.*

can produce immediate engagement. Top talent wants a solution and, when leadership is trusted or seen as an authentic partner, most will want to be part of developing the solution. Done well, this type of co-creation promotes *internal* talent-leadership buy-in and ownership that is necessary to address needs and create a win-win for the increasingly complex and growing problem of burnout and disengagement.

Co-branding: Co-branding is an *external* ownership of a product, service, or solution. In a business sense, it entails a client or customer promoting and being an ambassador for a product or organization that helped create a solution to solve a problem. The client or customer wants to be associated with the brand – their promotion is a form of co-branding. When top talent aligns with an organization and its leaders and wants to be associated with them, they will co-brand.

Top leaders understand the high value of co-branding. Co-branding is increasingly essential for talent referrals and acquisition. If an organization is not promoted by those within (and increasingly by those "formerly within"), that organization will be less successful or need to "pay up" to attract top talent. An organization's ability to differentiate itself in the marketplace is also becoming increasingly tied to co-branding as organizations are encouraged to show more of their "human side" and the unique aspects of their culture.

There is often a gap, however, in showing the human side – or at least authentically showing the human side – if the organization's only true focus is on the product, process, and bottom line. Being able to authentically co-impact on the job stimulates broader interest in co-branding and creates a much larger and expanded platform for showing the human side… another win-win.

Portability

Top talent wants the security of career portability. A winning brand and expanding platform provide this. The desired security does not rest solely in terms of having a job but also in terms of having the freedom to move to other opportunities that may be able to deliver more of what top talent wants.

Leaders and organizations that embrace and support a personal brand and platform will engender higher levels of trust, loyalty and ambassador support whether the employee remains with or eventually pivots away from an organization. Either way, this is a win-win. Leaders and organizations that cannot or choose not to be supportive of personal brands and platforms are best served by having open discussions with talent and then being supportive of a side-hustle or other out-of-the-office pursuits that allow for talents' greater and full development. This action demonstrates caring and respect and in turn provides a supportive pathway for trust and loyalty – yet another win-win.

Key Points

- Organizations and individuals are interested in establishing a winning brand and expanding platform. This mutual desire is a golden opportunity for organizations to create brand and platform alignment.
- Our brand is our story. It is what we want to represent and stand for – and it will very likely expand beyond our work identity.

- Our platform is the stage on which we perform and have impact at work and outside the office. Our platform needs to expand as we grow personally and professionally and transition to new seasons.
- Top talent has a new and expanded definition of winning that includes the traditional bottom line but goes far beyond it. Winning that attracts today involves more stakeholders, including top talent themselves and the communities in which we live, work, play, and serve.
- Where alignment exists, co-creation and co-branding is possible. Higher levels of engagement, buy-in, and ownership are possible with co-creation done well. Co-branding done well provides high value to organizations in terms of talent acquisition and marketplace differentiation.
- Organizations that create co-impact opportunities stimulate greater interest in co-branding.
- Top talent wants portability in terms of career, and having a winning brand and expanding platform helps provide that as well as the desired security.
- Leaders and organizations that embrace and support the building of a desired personal brand and platform – whether inside or outside the organization – will engender higher levels of trust, loyalty and

ambassador support whether the employee remains with or eventually pivots away from an organization.

A Winning Brand and Expanding Platform

Part 3:

Thriving in the New

We've covered the challenges and even the tragedy of burnout and disengagement and its impact on work and life today in the first part and defined the destinations that top talent seeks in Part 2. Now it's time to look at the blueprint and road map to face up to the challenge as individuals, organizations, and leaders and move toward the desired destination with a process that is designed to inspire, transform, and allow all to thrive.

Facing up to the challenges means directly taking on burnout and disengagement. We can halt the process and begin to unwind the burnout-disengagement cycle by addressing its components one-by-one, starting with our personal frustrations.

Addressing our personal frustrations requires us to want our lives to matter. To matter, we need to take a stand and take action to "resolve our busyness" as the first step to reversing burnout or avoiding it in the first place. Resolving our busyness means taking ownership of our time. As individuals, we need to own our time now with the same interest and passion we previously afforded our careers or businesses. Very simply, we need to master our time.

Addressing our work frustrations will require a little help from our organizations. For organizations to realize the benefits of engagement and growth, they must also want to matter. For organizations to become more relevant, they need to design their work and work environments to support, encourage, and enable top talent to win – the way they want to.

Leaders have a large and unmistakable role to play. The organization is the sum of leaders' ability to steward and grow the talent assets in their care. Leaders need to take a step back to reassess what it means to lead and what it means to shepherd resources to a greater destination. Leaders will need to determine whether they have the courage and the conviction to lead in ways that are relevant today. In the same way that top talent and organizations must want to matter, leaders must want to matter as well.

Chapter Seven:

Resolving Busy, Reversing Burnout

Reversing burnout, avoiding a recurrence, and avoiding it in the first place requires that we take personal responsibility for "mastering our life." We can begin by taking on our personal frustrations. These frustrations most often stem from missing out, so we need to choose to miss out no longer.

Mastering Our Time

Busyness is invasive and chokes out and overruns much what we desire in life. We need to resolve our busyness if we are to begin to master our lives. The first step is to take ownership and control of our time. When we control our time, we control our destiny.

To take control, we need to take action. For many of us, the first step is one of faith. We make the decision to take control without fully knowing or defining what exactly we want out of work and life. We may have known but have lost touch, track, and clarity. We may have known but have already checked the boxes of the goals that previously drove us. It is a step in faith because we may feel lost, disconnected, discontented, frustrated, and even resentful – especially if we are in or headed toward the burnout-disengagement cycle.

Taking control is a values-based decision because we need to value both ourselves and our time – possibly in new ways. As I explained in Chapter 4, many of us have invested so much in our careers that it has become our identity. But for most of us, "what we do" is not "who we are." Recall that most of us need to be able to expand beyond the office as it is today to live a full life and discover our life purpose. As we progress in life, the gap between what we are doing and who we are and our life purpose is what drives our discontent. Deciding to take control is a decision to value ourselves above our present discontent.

> **Taking control is a values-based decision; we need to value both ourselves and our time.**

Once we make the decision to resolve our discontent, we begin to value time itself with a greater sense of urgency. We realize that we are getting older. Our days are numbered on this earth and we have no real control of when our time will be up. Tomorrow is not guaranteed. Time is our greatest asset in terms of achieving our goals and realizing our impact, but we can't take it for granted. We know that we don't want to miss out any longer and that we may need a course correction. But here's the reality: We will never discover the things we value most and begin to track toward the full life we desire and our greater purpose until we slow down. In order to take control, we need to value our time enough to protect it and deploy it with great intention.

Once our time is suitably valued, we can design a system to master it. Mastering our time allows us to prioritize and systematically manage it in a way that propels us toward the future we desire. One of the essential elements of this system is to create "margin" – quiet time and personal "white space," away from devices and distractions – into our lives where we can gain clarity.

Clarity allows us to prioritize our work and life goals and better understand and identify our needs in terms of flexibility and the conditions we need to establish and to enforce boundaries necessary to balance and integrate goals. Gaining clarity, however, will require more than just rest and relaxation.

ELEMENTS TO MASTERING OUR TIME

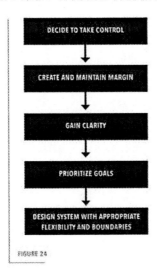

Figure 24 illustrates the elements to mastering our time.

R&R 2.0

The "rest and relaxation" of our past can help us address the physical demands of work and life, but it needs to be updated and expanded if we are going to take on burnout. The new version of R&R begins with the Restoration & Rediscovery phase.

Restoration – Rest and relaxation alone only address being physically or emotionally exhausted as a result of a temporary season or event. On the other hand, burnout is a chronic condition that layers frustration and loss, and even resentment and despair, on top of physical and emotional exhaustion. Reversing burnout requires a deeper and more strategic approach.

Restoration is the process of "getting us back to even." Once restored, we can move forward and toward our full potential. Using and maintaining the margin we create through mastering our time is the key to restoration. Margin needs to be designed well to be a true timeout and be sufficient in length and consistency. Well-designed margin allows us to routinely decompress, rest, pray, meditate, listen, think, contemplate, read, journal, and reflect.

Rediscovery – Margin is also foundational to rediscovery. Rediscovery is a process to become more self-aware – to understand who we are, where we stand, and what we stand for. Becoming more self-aware requires us to understand our seasons, our past, and our momentum. We can use the typical work-life seasons as well as the S-curve approach I presented in Chapter 2 as guides. Then we can take inventory and evaluate the "what" and the "how" of our life to date.

> *Sufficient margin is required for both Restoration and Rediscovery.*

We cannot rush rediscovery. It takes time and requires us to ask many "why's" as we go deeper into understanding the what and the how of our lives. As we work through the process, finding the why behind what we did or continue to do is important but not as important as finding the "who" behind the why. Finding our who – both who we are and who we serve – matters most. Who we are ties directly to our values, our wiring, and our purpose – the ultimate source of our interests, passions, and gifts. Who we serve ties to what we value today.

The Restoration & Rediscovery phase helps us understand and master our past and present. To master our future, we need to proceed onto the second phase of R&R 2.0.

Positioning for the Win

To position us to master our future to be able to win at work and life, R&R 2.0 proceeds to the Retargeting & Revitalization phase.

Retargeting – Retargeting is charting a new course for our future by setting a series of new destinations. These destinations are associated with our rediscovered interests, passions, and goals related to work and life appropriate with our seasons and the ultimate future we desire. For many of us, the destinations will include new targets for establishing and strengthening some of the key relationships needed for a full life that we did not make time for in the past.

The new course is the path we take to fill the gaps and side-step the traps and pitfalls between our present momentum and our desired future. The new course may require an adjustment to our current path and trajectory. In most cases, choosing what is most valuable will change the trajectory of our lives.

Revitalization – Revitalization is the positive state of mind and being we experience as we begin to take action toward our desired future. We master our future by acting today. A well-designed plan allows us to begin immediately from where we are and with what's in front of us. Our action could be at the office, outside of work, or as part of a side-hustle.

When we grow in self-awareness, we know more about what we want personally and professionally, and it is easier to act and begin to feel revitalized. Taking action also grows our social-awareness and overall emotional intelligence. This evolution increases our ability to purposefully align our brand and our platform with organizations that can help us win at both work and life – and thus help us master our life.

ELEMENTS TO MASTERING OUR LIFE

WINNING AT WORK	WINNING AT LIFE
Mastering Our Craft	Mastering Our Time
Making Our Name	Mastering Our Past and Present
Making a Difference	Mastering Our Future
Leaving a Legacy	Making Our Impact
	Inspiring Others

FIGURE 25

Figure 25 illustrates the elements to mastering our life.

Key Points

- We need to resolve our busyness if we want to begin to master our life. The first step to resolving our busyness is taking ownership and control of our time.
- Taking control of our time requires that we value ourselves and our finite time.
- Mastering our time allows us to design a system to prioritize and manage our goals.
- Creating and maintaining margin – quiet time and space without distraction – provides clarity in terms of goals and our need for flexibility and boundaries in achieving them.
- To reverse burnout, traditional rest and relaxation has been upgraded and expanded to R&R 2.0 with Restoration & Rediscovery to master our past and present and Retargeting & Revitalization to master our future.
- We master our future by acting today.

Chapter Eight

Designing Organizations to Matter

Organizations are either interested and committed to reversing burnout and reengaging talent... or they are not. If organizational management decides that they are onboard with reversing burnout and ultimately avoiding it from this point forward, they must act in ways that fully support reengagement of talent. Anything less than doing so is mere lip service and not only continues the burnout-disengagement cycle and the pivoting away of talent but actually greases the skids for those things to happen.

Growing discontent and pivoting trends demonstrate that top talent is taking their own initiative to design their lives and to position themselves to win. That many of those in the ranks of top talent are taking it upon themselves to figure out what they truly want and how to go about achieving it makes their organizations less relevant to their success, even making the prospect of disengagement and a pivot away more likely. For organizations to remain or become relevant to top talent, they need to matter and have greater significance to the very employees who are the foundation of the organization's success.

For organizations to matter, they need to take responsibility to effectively redesign work and the work environment to reduce prolonged overload and overwhelm and address any frustrations that contribute to burnout and disengagement. To matter moving forward, organizations need to enable greater impact – both inside and outside of the office.

Organizational Responsibility

Organizations that want to matter welcome the new. They see it as an opportunity to differentiate and grow – the same way leading edge companies see changes in the marketplace as opportunities rather than threats. Top organizations that understand the realities of work and life today will take responsibility for the work and work environment in order to enhance their success by engaging or reengaging their talented workforces. Similar to an individual *choosing* to control their time, organizations choosing to better control their success is a values-based decision. In this case, organizations *choose* to value their employees and the longer-term success of the organization in ever evolving and more relevant ways.

> *Successful organizations are those that want to matter and have impact, not simply be profitable.*

Organizations choosing to matter strive to create the conditions for employees to be fully engaged and excited to come to work and perform their roles and increase their contributions. These organizations will purposefully align with top talents' goals, interests, and passions and design co-learning, -creating, -impacting, and -branding opportunities with the goal to create thriving cultures and ensure needed buy-in and ownership by a fully engaged workforce.

Designing Impact

When I was actively researching and working through my burnout, disengagement, and side-hustles before ultimately deciding to pivot, I knew there was a better way, so I reversed engineered a process that, if in place at the time, would have kept me engaged in my former organization and career. Recall the discussion in Chapter 4: One of the keys to this process, and one of the keys to having fully engaged employees, is having work that provides continuous meaning and purpose.

Having work with meaning and purpose needs to be well planned to best meet the needs of the organization and its talent, be designed to be adaptable, and be well executed and maintained. The process I reverse engineered has I.M.P.A.C.T.™: Inventory, Mission, Plan, Authenticity, Capacity, Trigger

The I.M.P.A.C.T. process aligns with the layout of this book to ensure that the situation we are in and the destinations we seek are thoroughly understood and mapped as part of the process of taking action to move forward.

Inventory – The Inventory element is designed to let us know what's happening and where we stand. This step includes understanding: the presence and basis for any burnout and disengagement through well-designed questionnaires and interviews; the motivating interests, passions, and seasons of key employees through meetings and mapping; talent acquisition, retention, and growth results through evaluation and benchmarking; our market position and brand through the eyes of stakeholders, including customers, clients, or patients; and the tracking and evaluation of any present internal employee engagement and external impact-related activities and initiatives.

Mission – The Mission element is designed to articulate the reason our organization exists and provide targets. This step helps answer the questions: What inspires others about what we do and how we do it? What will attract top talent to join and stay in our organization? Is our mission, vision, and values statement aligned with what inspires and attracts... and do we live it daily? Does our

> *Organizational and employee awareness increases organizational intelligence.*

mission, vision, and values statement need to be expanded as part of expanding our platform in order to better attract and inspire?

Inventory and Mission elements are important in creating organizational self-awareness and employee-awareness and increase overall organizational emotional intelligence.

Plan – The Plan element is critical as it establishes the paths to take us from where we are now to our targets. Most organizations will benefit from having a third party involved in plan development. A qualified and experienced consultant will be able to identify readily achievable opportunities that we often lose sight of in our familiarity and our busyness within the organization. In terms of top talent engagement and growth, there is also much to understand on a macro-societal and across-industries scale that affects our organization that we often don't have the ability to perceive as a result of our close proximity to the issues. An outside party can share these perspectives and help assess how these can be leveraged for the benefit of both the organization and the workforce. An outside party can also facilitate a specific internal dialog and facilitate co-learning and co-creation of solutions to reverse and avoid burnout, restore efficacy, engage, and grow.

The ideal plan includes both internal and external targets. With so much daily time spent inside the office and in direct revenue-generating activities, our new growth is very likely to come from the outside and operating in new contexts and new environments. The good news is that this is exactly the type of experience top talent wants. The plan, however, must be designed in such a way that ensures that the experiences align to meet the mutual goals and targets.

Engagement and growth plans will best be designed to allow for new roles and experiences as well as networking and relationship building across the organization to decrease barriers and increase collaboration. The plan also targets emotional intelligence growth, and it also needs to be designed to support continuous engagement and growth through seasons and expanded definitions of success and winning.

> *Leading organizations use external impact to address burnout, engage and develop talent, and as a business growth strategy.*

External Impact

External impact is a movement that is leveraged by top organizations. Leading organizations leverage this by designing specific strategies to: address burnout, meet both internal and external engagement and development needs, and attract and differentiate itself in the marketplace. In addition to being part of the plan for I.M.P.A.C.T., external impact is a powerful and effective business growth strategy.

The idea of external impact resonates with most people today, including top talent, clients, customers, and the public at large. It resonates with organizational leaders, too, as a good thing to do… if only we knew what to do and had time the time to do it. As a result, this type of impact, for some, remains abstract – until leaders realize the benefits their organizations can enjoy by executing it effectively.

Why do some organizations hesitate to move forward with external impact? First, they don't fully understand what it is, what it can look like, and the benefits it can yield now and in the future.

> *Understanding external impact is the first step to realizing and enjoying its benefits.*

Without this understanding, status quo advocates seize and fill the void. When this happens, endless questions about needing to know all the costs and seeing a business case that ensures an immediate return quickly exhausts open-minded peers and "successfully" drains the life out of strategic planning and any true consideration of new approaches. Leading organizations seek to understand what are costs and what are actually wise investments, and navigate accordingly.

In some contexts, external impact has been termed "corporate social impact" (CSI), "corporate social responsibility" (CSR) or "corporate responsibility" (CR).

There are distinctions but for the purposes of this book, let's assume all to be associated with organizations looking to "do good" and "make a difference" externally while being responsive to the need to successfully operate and create high value and profits for the benefit of customers, employees, and other stakeholders. There is a broad range of activities that can be identified in these realms, and activities are often within environmental, social, or governance domains.

To share insight in the context of engagement and growth plan development, I'm taking a few paragraphs to include a brief overview of the external impact movement.

Archetypes of External Impact

A study was recently conducted to identify different archetypes of Fortune 500 companies related to external impact (Deloitte, 2015; reference 6). These archetypes included:

- "shareholder maximizers" representing only 11% of the companies,
- "corporate contributors" representing the majority at 53%,
- "impact integrators" representing a growing one-third at 33%, and
- "social innovators", the newest type, now representing 3%.

The "shareholder maximizers" were primarily represented by financial services and energy corporations.

The "corporate contributors" generally have programs or initiatives developed in response to external customer or internal employee desires to mitigate risk. In this setting, external contributions are often centralized and limited in terms of choice. They can also take the form of more siloed and disparate financial donations or volunteer efforts within the organizations.

The "impact integrators," on the other hand, were more internally motivated to achieve some sort of an external mission through the integration of business strategy and human capital, and worked across business units. In professional settings, integrating impact could involve designing staff engagement, development, and pro-bono activities more strategically and in ways that resonate both internally and externally.

The "social innovators" were more of the true social enterprises where the core mission is the business. Examples of these types of companies with which many of us may be familiar include Patagonia®, which has a mission to "...cause no unnecessary harm" and "use business to inspire and implement solutions to the environmental crisis" as well as TOMS® Shoes, which donates a pair of shoes for a child in need for every pair purchased.

For most businesses today, the opportunity to inspire others and differentiate in the marketplace lies with being more strategic and purposeful as a "corporate contributor" or moving toward becoming an "impact integrator."

The Window to Act

The "Theory of Diffusion of Innovation" helps explain how new technologies and social innovations spread within a population. If the Fortune 500 is a representative sample and a combined 36 percent of businesses as a whole can be defined as either "impact integrators" or "social innovators," then time is running short for most businesses to adapt from being "shareholder maximizers" or "corporate contributors" in order to maximize the benefits of effective external impact.

In terms of the Theory graphic presented, at 36 percent adoption of strategic impact, we are beyond the "innovators" (2.5%) and "early adopters" (13.5%) phases – often referred to as the "tipping point" (16%). We are well into the "early majority" phase and now poised for accelerated growth – especially since the "impact integrators," and the "social innovators" are seeing the greatest and fastest growth. Businesses looking to adapt within the "late majority" and "laggards" phases will be hard-pressed to leverage impact initiatives as a means to differentiate themselves internally and externally in the marketplace.

> *Organizations that integrate impact and socially innovate can more easily differentiate themselves.*

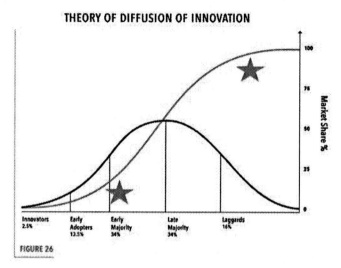

FIGURE 26

Figure 26 illustrates the potential growth of the spread of corporate social impact for "impact integrators" and "social innovators" versus all other archetypes except "shareholder maximizers."

Even today, it is much harder to impress, inspire, or "wow" top talent, clients or other stakeholders if we are only able to align with the 89 percent of organizations that can also claim corporate social impact (i.e., all less the "shareholder maximizers").

Effective External Impact Works

A recent study quantified the added value of effective external impact to successfully run businesses (Project ROI, IO Sustainability, 2015; reference 7). For businesses in the Standard & Poor (S&P) 500, overall value increased four to six percent, revenue and pricing power increased up to 20 percent, staff retention increased up to 50 percent, and productivity increased up to 13 percent. The study also found "that strong 'corporate responsibility' programs' performance increases the commitment, affinity, and engagement of employees. This in turn enhances job performance, increases productivity, reduces turnover, lowers absenteeism, and even reduces the incidences of employee corruption. In addition, employee engagement links to 'corporate responsibility' programs in a virtuous cycle. Together they reinforce one another and enhance financial performance, sales revenue, brand and reputational value, and innovative capability."

We are now midway through outlining the I.M.P.A.C.T. process. This is the "get real" and "get honest" part for leaders and organizations. Without **Authenticity**, **Capacity**, and the courage to pull the **Trigger**, our results will fall short. It is at this point where we, as leaders and as a leadership team, may need to take action ourselves.

As a sidebar: In order to successfully preside over I.M.P.A.C.T., we may need to first confirm or simultaneously establish these elements "internally" as an individual and as a leadership team through a separate but related process. I developed this as the A.C.T.^{TM} process, which is a combination of the Authenticity, Capacity, and Trigger elements outlined below and the "mastering" principles I presented in Chapter 7.

Authenticity – The Authenticity element is designed to ensure we have the credibility as leaders and organizations to succeed in the new. Authenticity in leadership is critical to success today. Authenticity cannot be manufactured – it is how others see, experience, and trust our actions and intentions. As leaders, our self-awareness and overall level of emotional intelligence are key to being authentic, but – as we covered previously – the reality is as individuals and organizational leaders we, on average, *lose* emotional intelligence as we succeed in our careers. In a number of cases, an important step in the process will be to re-establish personal and organizational awareness and work to better align or realign brands and platforms to achieve needed levels of authenticity to succeed.

Capacity – The Capacity element is designed to ensure that we can successfully support and execute the plan. It includes individual and organizational capacity through allocating time, appropriately prioritizing, and educating, supporting, encouraging, and enabling action. Engagement and impact activities and initiatives cannot be "one more thing to do." We cannot "volun-tell" someone what to do without providing a path and benefit over the long term. The presence of burnout and disengagement limits and eliminates capacity; therefore, it needs to be reversed in order to be successful.

Trigger – The Trigger element is designed to establish a framework and work through the logistics and steps necessary for triggering action to achieve the plan. Since we may be breaking from our conventional past to realize the promise of a better future, triggering action takes some degree of courage. If we are not authentic with the need to adapt to the new or are not truly committed to creating the capacity and doing what is necessary to successfully execute the plan, a hesitation to act is normal. Sweeping action is not necessary from the start. In fact, it is best to start with small, but consistent steps as part of the larger plan to build engagement and momentum and gather feedback. By triggering action, however, top leaders and organizations send the message that they fear the consequences of staying the same and fear missing out on a new and better future in which they can excel beyond the short-term comfort of the status quo.

Key Points

- Organizations need to decide if they are interested in and committed to reversing burnout and engaging talent. If yes, anything less than new action continues the burnout-disengagement cycle and the pivoting away of talent.
- For organizations to matter moving forward, they need to enable greater impact – both inside and outside of the office.
- Employee engagement requires work with meaning and purpose which needs to be well planned, designed, executed, and maintained.
- The I.M.P.A.C.T. process is designed to immediately engage top talent and generate growth.

- Done effectively, external impact is a strategy that can be designed to be leveraged to meet both internal and external engagement and growth goals – and provide an opportunity to attract and differentiate.

Chapter Nine:

Courage to Win and Transform the American Workplace

As a leader, am I part of the problem or the solution? Is the problem someone else's fault and someone else's to solve? Are the issues beyond my comprehension and ability to act? Do I care more about maintaining the focus and making the numbers than making a plan to reverse burnout and engage top talent? Am I afraid of straying from convention?

Momentum is a powerful force. Conventional industrial-era thinking continues to exact a price on many of us as individuals, organizations, communities... and even as a nation. Somebody needs the courage to take a stand. It will first be a person – a leader – who begins the process and propels momentum in a new direction. Are you that leader? Is your boss or someone else in the organization a leader who will step up? Or is it a peer in another organization who will have the courage to move past the old and begin to thrive in the new?

Finding the Courage

Leaders are on notice and need to act to remain relevant personally and positionally. Just as the realities of work and life today have created loss, so will it be in the new. This time, however, the losses won't be felt by top talent – and they won't be felt by those with the courage to matter. The loss will be felt by those who fail to understand the true impact of burnout... and their organizations.

Fear the Status Quo – Our obligation as leaders is to look toward the future and ensure we have a path to get from "here" to "there" in the best possible way. Administering busyness and managing the "here" only fortifies our present momentum – the one that ultimately carries us to burnout and disengagement. Even if the going is good, the good eventually slows, peaks, and declines without a well-designed refresh or pivot. Recall, if you will, the S-curve we covered in Chapter 2. Without a refresh, it's a continuous and potentially precipitous decline. Leaders who merely ride the curve have much to fear beyond the horizon.

Top leaders will seek to understand their organization's past and present momentum and look to the future. Even if a "peak" may seem far in the distance, new targets will need to be locked in to avoid an otherwise inevitable decline. To attract, engage, grow, and retain top talent, effective leaders will target bold initiatives and avoid approaches that only "tweak" the present.

> *You're either growing and moving forward or declining and moving backward.*

Tweaking things that are broken, frankly, is a cop out. If something is broken enough to result in noticeable burnout, disengagement, pivoting away, or the inability to attract top outside talent, tweaking won't fix those issues. Tweaking is usually a tactic to appease change advocates in a way that actually does little to disrupt the status quo. Without being part of a committed-to, grander plan, "bolt-on" initiatives often get buried and lost in the busyness and the day-to-day and end up doing more harm than good. This is especially true when issues resurface again and advocates (and those affected) are more burned-out, disengaged, and closer to a pivot. Failure to solve important issues undermines leaders' credibility, and leads top talent to question the leaders' effectiveness or even fitness for the position. "Starting small" toward a new and bolder destination with embedded authenticity and capacity, on the other hand, is much different.

Decide to Matter – As leaders, we matter… if we decide and choose to. We abdicate our responsibility and diminish our impact when we are lost in our busyness and lost on our team. If we are *true* leaders, we need to step up, assume our position, and fulfill our mandate. If we occupy a leadership position for vanity or static- or self-interest, we need to step down and pursue another path – one better aligned with our calling so as not to be personally and organizationally rejected by top talent.

True leaders are gifted and appointed to serve others and help manifest a better future and a greater good. True leaders have an inner drive and conviction to serve, grow, and create – even if the ambition to do so has been repressed or is just beginning to emerge. Like a river, true leaders refuse to be held back. If not truly engaged in their work as a greater calling, rightful leaders will flow around or build up behind and naturally push through blockages or begin to flow in a new direction, bypassing or sweeping away the ideas of ineffectual leadership.

In deciding to matter as a leader, we need to commit to growing in self-, social-, work-, employee-, and marketplace-awareness to sharpen our vision and understand more of our purpose. Our pursuit and discovery of awareness and embracing our best role in realizing the vision is our authenticity – and is what inspires and engages top talent in the mission.

Leading the Win

Top leaders are vested in learning what it takes to win in the new. Top leaders are spearheading and pulling the trigger on new approaches to address today's realities rather than relying on antiquated thinking or embracing the status quo.

Know the Game – Today's game is about the talent and is played above the bottom line. In professional services and in most businesses, the clients and customers cannot be served and the profit cannot be made or sustained without the talent. The organization also cannot be sold or transferred at high values without the talent. It's about the talent. It's about the talent. It's. About. The. Talent.

The object of the game is to adapt all the major technological changes and evolving workplace and marketplace expectations to something that really hasn't changed – the person – the talent. The employee as a person has been stretched, bent, and even broken, but has not – and will not – change in terms of fundamental needs and a desire for a full life with impact and significance. Leaders who authentically and deftly engage top talent in redesigning the workplace for winning by fully understanding these needs will win themselves.

Set the Stage – Top leaders will set the stage for winning by creating and supporting a culture of excellence and trust. In so doing, top leaders can earn the trust of employees through designing engagements to connect, align, and coach, and by ensuring psychological safety. Psychological safety is present in settings in which talent is free to share ideas, speak from the heart, and take appropriate risks without judgment in pursuit of success, knowing their team and boss have their back.

Top leaders will also extend trust by providing flexibility in terms of schedules and appropriate margin to reverse and ward-off burnout with full confidence that it will lead to greater loyalty and a greater capacity for top talent to perform at high levels over a longer, more sustainable period – and do so with higher levels of engagement.

Trigger I.M.P.A.C.T. – By trigging the I.M.P.A.C.T. process described in Chapter 8, leaders send a clear message that they recognize the realities of today and that they care and want to move forward and create a better future for all. They realize that in addition to a thriving culture, they need to allow for and provide impact. The I.M.P.A.C.T. process is designed to immediately engage and advance co-learning, co-creation, and growth opportunities, as well as the opportunity to begin the transformation in small steps designed to build further engagement and momentum toward the win.

As I mentioned in Chapter 8, leaders and leadership teams may need to confirm or establish the Authenticity, Capacity, and Trigger elements to most effectively leverage I.M.P.A.C.T. on an organizational level. This can be accomplished through the A.C.T. process. Solidifying these elements may be applicable to leaders who themselves are dealing with forms of burnout. This process may also be applicable for leaders and leadership teams looking to establish their place and win in the new as fast and as smooth as possible.

Key Points

- Courage is needed to counter antiquated conventional thinking and transform the workplace to reverse burnout, engage top talent, and grow.
- Leaders can find courage to act by fearing the status quo and deciding to truly matter.
- Leaders can fulfill their mandate by becoming vested in the new and championing a process designed for both organizations and talent to win.
- Focusing on what will also enable talent to excel, building a culture of excellence and trust, and trigging A.C.T. and I.M.P.A.C.T. processes are positive steps top leaders are using to win. Join them.

What's Next

I hope that I've helped you to more fully understand burnout and its impact on top talent and organizations. I also hope that I've been able to provide you with answers on how to reverse burnout, immediately engage top talent and grow, and in the process do our part to transform the American workplace for the benefit of us all.

I welcome your comments and thoughts. Please reach out to me personally at pete@actionsprove.com or visit us at www.actionsprove.com to schedule a time to strategize on how I can help you and your organization win today through:

- Coaching,
- Consulting,
- Training,
- Impact Tracking, and
- Speaking.

More details at: www.actionsprove.com/what-we-do/

Become part of our ActionsProve community at http://www.reversingburnoutbook.com/community/ to receive a free gift and be notified of new content and upcoming events.

Please also Follow, Like, Share, and Connect with us on social media.

References & Resources:

1. Kronos Incorporated and Future Workplace, 2017. "The Employee Burnout Crisis: Study Reveals Big Workplace Challenge in 2017."
https://www.kronos.com/about-us/newsroom/employee-burnout-crisis-study-reveals-big-workplace-challenge-2017

2. Gallup, 2017. "State of the American Workplace Report."
http://news.gallup.com/reports/199961/state-american-workplace-report-2017.aspx

3. Corporate Global Challenge, 2016. "The Cost of Presenteeism – and How to Fix it."
https://globalchallenge.virginpulse.com/blog/the-cost-of-presenteeism

4. Bradberry, Travis, and Jean Greaves. *Emotional Intelligence 2.0: the World's Most Popular Emotional Intelligence Test*. TalentSmart, 2009.

5. *Harvard Gazette*, 2017. "Good genes are nice, but joy is better": Harvard study, almost 80 years old, has proved that embracing community helps us live longer, and be happier.
https://news.harvard.edu/gazette/story/2017/04/over-nearly-80-years-harvard-study-has-been-showing-how-to-live-a-healthy-and-happy-life/

6. Deloitte, 2015. "Driving corporate growth through social impact - Four corporate archetypes to maximize your social impact."
https://www2.deloitte.com/us/en/pages/operations/articles/driving-corporate-growth-through-social-impact.html

7. IO Sustainability, 2015. "Project ROI – Defining the Competitive and Financial Advantages of Corporate Responsibility and Sustainability."
http://iosustainability.com/programs/project-roi/

Other Resources Cited:

Buford, Bob. *Halftime: Moving from Success to Significance*. Zondervan, 2015.

Corbett, Steve, and Brian Fikkert. *When Helping Hurts: How to Alleviate Poverty without Hurting the Poor ... and Yourself.* Moody Publishers, 2012.

Lupton, Robert D. *Toxic Charity: How Churches and Charities Hurt Those They Help (and How to Reverse It)*. HarperCollins, 2011.

About the Author

Peter Atherton is a talented and accomplished consultant, speaker, and author with over 24 years of experience as a successful professional engineer, executive, and business owner. Pete currently serves as the President and Founder of ActionsProve, LLC (www.actionsprove.com). ActionsProve teams with businesses and professionals to create greater growth and profits through more effective employee engagement, retention, and impact initiatives through consulting, training, and coaching.

From the beginning of his career, and for more than two decades, Pete has demonstrated that he is a high achiever, gaining professional success and standing on an accelerated path. Pete is a highly skilled and accomplished professional engineer (designing sophisticated public infrastructure and water treatment systems) and was a senior executive, a major firm owner, and member of his firm's Board of Directors.

Along the way, Pete received the Younger Civil Engineer of the Year Award from the Maine Section of the American Society of Civil Engineers.

During Pete's tenure as a senior executive, his firm doubled its staff and tripled its revenue. The firm had also been recognized by several industry organizations for its strong growth and business operations. The firm was included in *Engineering News Record* (ENR) magazine's Top 500 Design Firms and their Top 200 Environmental Design Firms in the country and was ranked in the nation's top 25 for wastewater engineering. *Inc.* magazine rated the firm as one the 500 fastest growing firms in the country in 2010. PSMJ, a firm dedicated to the marketing and development of Architecture/Engineering firms worldwide, regularly awarded the firm their annual "Circle of Excellence Award" after assessing benchmarks for operations, management and sustainability.

In what was initially a "parallel life" to his work that began in his early 30s, Pete has served in the nonprofit and community development sector for over a dozen years. In addition to holding board positions, Pete has co-led approximately 20 international service teams and resource development initiatives, plus the design and construction of numerous infrastructure projects, the development of a social enterprise farm business, and the development of educational programs. Pete has also co-founded chapters of 100 Men Who Care in Southern Maine and Knoxville, Tennessee.

Outside of work and service, Pete has been blessed with a fulfilling family life and was recently able to experience the challenges and the joys of beginning anew, empty-nesting with his wife.

At the age of 40, and at what would be considered the peak of his career, Pete designed and initiated a multi-year exit strategy to pivot toward a life with greater meaning and purpose. In 2016, he founded ActionsProve to converge his love for business, people, problem solving, and systems design to help individuals and organizational leaders achieve greater results and also have greater impact and significance.

Pete obtained his Bachelor of Science degree in civil engineering from the University of New Hampshire. He holds an Executive Certificate in Transformational Nonprofit Leadership from the University of Notre Dame Mendoza College of Business. He completed other engineering, management, and entrepreneurial coursework from Worcester Polytechnic Institute and Northeastern University. Pete is also an avid self-learner, regularly attending conferences and participating in master-mind groups.